the dating race

the dating race

*An Undercover Report from the Front Lines
of Modern-Day Romance*

stacy kravetz

Jeremy P. Tarcher / Penguin

a member of Penguin Group (USA) Inc.

New York

JEREMY P. TARCHER/PENGUIN

Published by the Penguin Group

Penguin Group (USA) Inc., 375 Hudson Street, New York, New York 10014, USA •
Penguin Group (Canada), 10 Alcorn Avenue, Toronto, Ontario, Canada M4V 3B2 (a division of
Pearson Penguin Canada Inc.) • Penguin Books Ltd, 80 Strand, London WC2R 0RL, England • Penguin
Ireland, 25 St Stephen's Green, Dublin 2, Ireland (a division of Penguin Books Ltd) • Penguin Group
(Australia), 250 Camberwell Road, Camberwell, Victoria 3124, Australia (a division of Pearson Australia
Group Pty Ltd) • Penguin Books India Pvt Ltd, 11 Community Centre, Panchsheel Park,
New Delhi–110 017, India • Penguin Group (NZ), Cnr Airborne and Rosedale Roads, Albany,
Auckland 1310, New Zealand (a division of Pearson New Zealand Ltd) • Penguin Books
(South Africa) (Pty) Ltd, 24 Sturdee Avenue, Rosebank, Johannesburg 2196, South Africa

Penguin Books Ltd, Registered Offices: 80 Strand, London WC2R 0RL, England

Library of Congress Cataloging-in-Publication Data
Kravetz, Stacy.
The dating race: an undercover report from the front lines
of modern-day romance / Stacy Kravetz.
p. cm.
ISBN 1-58542-400-5
1. Dating (Social customs). 2. Man-woman relationships. 3. Courtship. I. Title.
HQ801.K72 2005 2004058077
306.73—dc22

Printed in the United States of America
1 3 5 7 9 10 8 6 4 2

Book design by Meighan Cavanaugh

for jay,

my last blind date

acknowledgments

A special thank-you to the following people who put me in touch with great interviewees and to those who shared their dating trials and tribulations: Jake Baskin, Bobby Bell, Jon Burke, Katherine Butler, Sheryl Craig Cooper, Will Dodson, Steve Druker, John Eddow, Patti Fullerton, Andrea Gellert, Risa Gertner, Jay A. Goldberg, Jay M. Goldberg, Phyllis Goldberg, Renae Goldberg, Mo Hafez, Heather Hartt, Susie Helfrey, Elizabeth Herrick, Jack Herrick, Tricia Herrick, Jennifer Heyman, Paula Hidalgo, Vandy Howell, Dunniela Kaufman, Leah Keith, Dana Kravetz, Joanne Kravetz, Tony Lam, Linda Lea, Rich Lester, Rosemary Lichtman, David Light, Tim Marema, Amy McCubbin, Denise McDonald, Michelle Morrow, Oliver Muoto, Micki Pagano, Jason Pair, Tony Parente, Carlos Pianelli, Richard Rabkin, Marni Rosen, Judie Rosenman, Craig Russell, Steve Ruth, Nancy Sheffner, Jeff Sinaiko, Michael Sloan, Laura Sohn, Jennifer Sweet, Stacy Tenenbaum, Katie Thurer, Mike Trozzo, and Abby Wolf-Weiss.

Thank you to Jonathan Abrams, Priscilla Chang, Malcolm Parks, and Edward Hallowell for valuable insights into our culture of dating and to Bill Glass for top-notch statistical research.

To my agent, Alice Martell, the earliest fan of this project: thank you for helping me redirect the book's focus and for never losing faith. And thank you to Trish Hall for putting us in touch. To Sara Carder at

Penguin, an insightful editor who encouraged me to stay true to my original concept of the book.

To my parents, Bryan Kravetz and Joanne Kravetz, thank you for always supporting my choice of career and for (mostly) sparing me your own dating stories. And to my brother, Dana, for doing battle in the dating trenches and living to tell about it. Thanks also for giving me notes on the first draft.

Most of all, to my husband, Jay Goldberg, for being completely unflappable while I was doing my research and for being there with love at the end of every day. And to Jesse, who doesn't think girls are yucky.

contents

the dating race

introduction

no one said dating was easy

♥

♥

♥

Los Angeles, California

Mindy, forty-one years old, posts her profile on Yahoo! Personals with a provocative personal statement: "'People are more fun than anybody.' So said Miss Dorothy Parker and I have found it to be true. I am very eclectic. I enjoy films, music, books, gardening, KCRW and work peripherally in the entertainment industry. I like talking to people, especially if they are smart, funny, courteous, and engaged in the world. My objective is to meet people; if this leads to romance—so be it."

Within a few days she begins corresponding with a man she dubs Punk Gardener.

She writes, "Okay, you are clearly in the advanced home-owner league. As a minor leaguer (just 2 years) I am still planting and then moving the plants around the yard. Your garden sounds more like crops. I have a very teeny homestead and painted (with my Dad and sister) the entire interior when I moved in. I was glad to hear from you."

"Howdy," he writes back. "Winter Rye, yea I kinda want some lawn this year, when I moved in I planted fruit trees (Apple, Orange, 2 Pomegranates) and they have grown to the point that I get hardly any direct sunlight in the backyard. When I bought my house I did the same as you, I enlisted the help of all the family I could bribe. Within 3 weeks I had the place painted, holes in walls patched etc. It was quite a project but it is mine. Take it easy."

Mindy replies, "What kind of dog is Rosie—have you had her a long time? What are your current musical likes—I know that it was punk but is that still your current taste, or have other styles filtered in over the years? I have a garage in which I revive nothing. I like dogs but do not have one. I like a lot of different kinds of music—I am a mood listener. Your turn."

Punk Gardener responds, "Let's see, I have a garage I use for woodworking and car fixing. My pup Rosie is a German Shepherd mix. She's very smart and very sweet. As far as music goes, that's kinda tough cuz' I don't really like much of what I hear on the radio these days, I could go on about that one for a while, but maybe another time. Gotta get back to work right now."

The correspondence lasts a month before the first phone conversation. They talk for hours. Mindy and Punk Gardener make plans to meet. She has a good feeling about him—they seem to share the same interests and have an easy banter on the phone.

Another month goes by. The two finally make plans for an in-person date, but at the last minute, Punk Gardener cancels. He doesn't say why; he doesn't reschedule. Mindy never hears from him again.

Toronto, Canada

Richard is struggling with his *shadchan*, the Orthodox Jewish matchmaker who has been sending him out on dates, seemingly without regard for his taste in women. He protests. The discussions about his standards escalate into fights. "She'll say I should give girls more of a chance, but I know after one date whether or not I am interested. If I'm not into it, I don't want to go out again. But in the religious community they frown on going out once and saying 'I'm out,'" he says.

"I said to the *shadchan*, 'I don't want you setting me up with unattractive girls.' There was silence on the phone. I asked, 'Is that controversial?' And she said, 'Actually it is. One person could look at a painting and hate it and another could look at the same painting and think it was lovely. I want to speak to one of your rabbis,'" the *shadchan* tells Richard.

The *shadchan* calls Richard back a minute later, crying. "You put up walls and I'm just trying to break them down," she tells Richard.

"This is the woman who is supposed to be helping me find a relationship and I am having relationship issues with her," Richard says. "It was time to take a break." He hasn't spoken to her in more than three months.

Whitesburg, Kentucky

In an old coal-mining town in rural Kentucky, Laura is among the minority for having gone away to college and for still being single at age twenty-five. Whitesburg is a conservative part of the country, with virtually no cultural or ethnic diversity among the 1,200 residents. The economy of the area is poor. There are no coffee shops or grocery stores. The closest movie theater is 75 miles away. Laura and the friends she works with all have a similar background: white, middle class, college educated. And they spend most of their time together. "There's a bar twenty miles from here where we do go out," she says, "but none of us has had a date there. It has to do with class and education. People tend to stay within groups that are tightly defined by class. Those are the people who make up our comfort zones.

"People here get married very young, and also get divorced very young. You find that, in poverty-stricken areas, people tend to get married young and have kids. I'm one of two people from my high school who hasn't gotten married yet." Laura has a boyfriend whom she met through friends of his from college. He's from central Kentucky and moved to Whitesburg after he and Laura started dating. "More often," she says, "people from here end up moving away to where their partner is. It's a special person who wants to live here." Laura and her boyfriend have been dating for two years.

New York City

Amelia sits down at a bar on a dark snowy street somewhere between Times Square and Chelsea. It's just a neighborhood Irish pub with a smattering of wood-hewn tables and bottles of every conceivable liquor displayed in front of a mirrored wall behind the bar. A guy who looks about thirty sits down next to Amelia and smiles. She smiles back. He picks up a small white card from a stack provided by the bar. On it he writes, "Hi. I'm Jim."

Amelia picks up another white card from the stack and introduces herself. Other than the sound of a mellow Bob Marley song leaking from a jukebox in the middle of the room, the bar is quiet. Amelia and Jim are two of about one hundred participants at a Quiet Party, an event where all conversations take place on paper.

"I like the idea of a mellower scene," Amelia says. At the end of the night, after writing notes for three hours with different people, some of which consist merely of the kind of lewd pickup lines that soured her on the traditional bar scene in the first place, Amelia is ready to go home. "I met some interesting people but none that I really want to go out with. Maybe next time," she says.

Los Angeles, California

Karen's work schedule is demanding. She's a doctor and has long shifts at a local hospital, but she admits she could make more time for dating if she wanted to. "I maybe use work as a crutch or an excuse not to be more active," says Karen, a gay woman originally from Miami. She has the most success meeting potential partners at parties hosted by other gay friends. "Otherwise it's a case of someone setting me up with the only other lesbian they know." But even trying to meet women through her friends is daunting: "The effort, the prepping is exhausting," she says. "You go to these parties and have to impress a whole group of people. And you realize there are not that many people out there for you, and you can't meet the people you want to meet." Sometimes it's easier to stay home.

"I've always known I wanted to be with someone," says Karen, thirty-one. "Right around the time I turned thirty, I started to feel the pressure." Some of that pressure revolves around having children. "It's going to be a hassle however I decide to have kids," she says. "It's going to be a production, no matter what."

Karen moves across town and starts a new job. She's feeling a little lonely, and it motivates her to get proactive about dating. She signs up for three online dating services and looks into a speed-dating event. She goes on a blind date but there's no chemistry. So she's open to it when a friend offers to set her up with someone else. "By the third date I realized I had a crush," she says. Karen and her girlfriend continue dating for eight months.

St. Louis, Missouri

Mike opens the car door for Abby at the beginning of their date, and she settles into the passenger seat of his gray Mustang. They drive to a nice Italian restaurant in St. Louis where Mike hopes to impress Abby with his knowledge of wine and food. The maître d' escorts Mike and Abby to a quiet red leather booth in the back where they can talk for hours. Along with Abby's brother and her sister.

Such are the dating requirements for Abby and Mike, both American children of Muslim families, who expect them to adhere to certain traditions. Abby's sister and brother accompany Mike on the first few dates so it won't feel socially improper for Abby to be seen in public with a man. Mike is a grad student, so he's chronically short on cash, but on their dates he's expected to pay for Abby and her siblings. "After a while it started to get really expensive, but it's just what you have to do if you want to date properly," Mike says.

After a half-dozen chaperoned dates, Mike tells Abby he'd like to see her alone. That means he has to state his intentions to her and to her parents: "I'd like to date you with the goal of getting married," he says.

Abby and her parents accept. When Abby's sister hears about Mike's plans, she bows four times in prayer. Ordinarily only two bows are customary but she gladly exceeds the expectation. Mike is pleased. At this point, he also formally asks Abby's family if he can take her out on dates as a precursor to marriage. Abby's mother calls the friends she has in town and asks them to check him out. "It's a small community," Mike says. "Her friends would not have a hard time finding someone who knows someone who knows me." Abby's mother's friend reports back that Mike is an upstanding guy. Abby and Mike go out alone together on their first date.

kingdom *animalia*, class *insecta*

Down beneath some bright green foliage, a certain male praying mantis is especially hopeful. He spies a female basking on a leaf nearby. She has long legs, stick-straight posture, and some healthy color in her face. The male mantis freezes, plotting how to woo her. He looks around in the surrounding leaves. The female appears to be alone. No other mantis females giggling in a group and discussing office politics over a drop of water. No other mantis male standing nearby, carrying her purse. And she's not wearing a wedding band. He gets excited. She could be the one.

The male mantis cautiously moves closer, careful not to scare her away. When he gets within range, insect instinct takes over. He skips the pleasantries, jumps on her, and begins to mate furiously. Afternoon sex in the sun, and he doesn't even know her name.

Moments later, the female tires of this game. She twists around, bites off his head, and eats it, forever putting to rest the question of a second date.

no one said dating was easy

In countless restaurants in cities across the country, men and women are munching on plates of field greens with pear-balsamic infusion and raising glasses of house merlot to toast the hope of a romantic future. At countless desktops, the Web savvy are logging into online dating sites and scrolling though the new candidates—with pictures—hoping to find someone worthy of an introductory e-mail. And in their precious spare time, countless hopeful men and women are attending dating seminars, reading the latest mate-snaring guides and speed-dating their way through coffee with a dozen new romantic candidates in under an hour.

The state of dating today is the state of our lives today: we work long hours and have increasingly little free time; we live in a service economy where we are accustomed to hiring others to do things for us; we live in a culture where businesses spring up to fill any perceived need; we marry later and date longer, often feeling an urgency by the time we are ready to meet "the one"; and we spend less time on the dates themselves, attempting to make quick decisions about their viability before investing more time. In 2002 there were more than fifty-one million adults over age eighteen who've never been married, or 24 percent of all adults over eighteen, according to the U.S. Census Bureau.

Dating as we know it has its roots in the early twentieth century. The working classes led the shift as a matter of practicality: they lived in urban areas and didn't have homes with parlors for courting. They dated in public places and were soon followed by the wealthier classes who envied the autonomy from prying eyes of family. Technological changes brought movie theaters, automobiles, and telephones, all of which gave men and women more freedom in their dating lives. Dating gave rise to new issues— namely, who would pay when a date consisted of going out for food and entertainment? Today the issues are how to meet each other in the first place.

We spent nearly $1 billion on matchmaking services in 2003, with a 9 percent increase expected for 2004, according to MarketResearch.com, an online research compiler. That's a stack of one-dollar bills 62.5 miles high, or about half the proposed 2004 budget for the state of Delaware.

Let's face it, most of us are not out there dating for the fun and frivolity of it all. We have a purpose: to search for love, no matter how difficult the process or slim the prospects may seem at the end of a particularly grueling first date. The quest for love is one of our most basic drives. We search for love as a way of developing bonds with each other, as a way of gaining emotional security, and ultimately as a way of perpetuating the species. Our search for love begins with a single date, whether arranged by a family matriarch or sought out through an Internet matching service. But love has never seemed so elusive.

Thanks to our ancestors who did away with arranged marriages, we're searching for love unfettered by the puritanical mandate that gave parents the power and duty to find appropriate matches for their children. During those times, a man who tried to court without permission could be sued by a girl's father. Marriages weren't about love and romance. They were about land, dowries, and power. But those prerogatives changed mid-nineteenth century when men and women began choosing their own romantic partners. Love became the only acceptable basis for marriage. It still is. And now we're at a loss for how to find it.

Courtship rituals have come a long way from the Victorian era of romantic messages spelled out in flower bouquets and minuets designed to introduce new partners as they swooned to classical music. That's not to say that flowers and ball gowns represent the right way to date and computer terminals and speed-dates are a turn for the worse. Our dating rituals simply reflect our times. And in these times, dating is not the delicate courtship ritual it used to be.

part one

low-tech dating

"It's not really until you hit thirty that you start to feel the pressure to get married," says James. But then he runs through a mental list of his friends from college and realizes he's one of a handful who isn't married. James is twenty-four. Two of his college roommates got married during college, and most of the rest married their college sweethearts immediately after their years at Baylor College in Houston, Texas. "Once you get out of college, it's a totally different ball game," James says. "I don't feel super pressure to get married. I'm involved in trying to meet someone, but it's not like I'm a headhunter or anything."

All the same, James would like to marry within the Christian faith, and the small Texas town where James teaches Latin at a university is 350 miles away from the network of family and friends where he grew up. So the church is his primary resource. Regular Sunday worship services don't provide a chance to socialize in and of themselves, James says. It feels awkward trying to strike up conversations after services when the purpose is to worship, not to cruise for dating opportunities. James meets more people at church study groups, where men and women discuss scripture and socialize in a more informal way after Sunday services. "If I'm outside the church setting, it will take three or four dates to find out about a girl, whereas in college you'd know everything about everyone," James says.

James's church group has the benefit of drawing together people with similar values and interests, and it takes the pressure off of meeting new people. "The church is like college. The screening process doesn't take as long, and it's even more exclusive than the academic setting because I'm around people who have a similar bond," James says. The church group functions like a community, because it recreates an academic setting where James can get to know women in some kind of context other than sitting across the table over a pizza. "It's such an intimate setting when you study scripture that it acts as a screening process," he says. "You learn about what someone's values are, her world view. You see how people carry themselves, what they talk about. Outside that, how else would you know?"

Here are a few little things that greatly lessen a woman's charm in most men's eyes:

Red hands or arms.
Finger nails too highly polished or shaped like swords.
Fat women with bobbed hair.
Hair that is "doctored" in any way.
Cheap perfumes.
Whiney voices.
Giggling.
Earrings like chandeliers.
Knickers in the city.

FROM *This Passion Called Love*, BY ELINOR GLYN, 1925

1.

singles events—
the almost aborted
mixer mission

♥

♥

♥

I sign up for a "Lock and Key" party, wondering if I will be inadvertently wandering into a fraternity party for over-the-hill college students lacking better ways of starting up a conversation. In fact, the lock-and-key premise seems to have come straight out of college, where I distinctly remember a subtly named "screw your buddy" party in which men carried around screws, women carried nuts, and the object was to achieve a not-so-subtle version of a snug fit. My nut was painted pink and I never did find the appropriate match.

At the post-college version, women carry around locks and men grasp clammy hands around tiny keys, in keeping with the image of men looking for a place to insert their hardware. And using the potential to unlock as an icebreaker, the conversations are certain to ensue. Each time a man and woman successfully identify the matching lock and key, they get a raffle ticket for prizes to be given out later. The more matches, the more opportunities to win things like a photo session for "lookbetteronline.com," tickets to speed-dating events, or admission to future Lock and Key parties. Apparently, the more successful we are at being single, the more opportunities for continued singles socializing we can come by.

It turns out I have to be fairly organized to receive my share of imploring keys. The party requires online registration with the option of prepayment. I go to the organization's Web site, where I can look at event photos and read testimonials about how much fun past Lock and Key parties have been. I study the photos of men and women smiling and holding drinks, wearing their locks and keys around their necks below their red-and-white name tags. Some have apparently found their match, with keys poised to open their requisite locks. When I look closer, I notice a woman in a slinky purple dress in four different pictures and another voluptuous woman in a low-cut top, who appears in three photos. Perhaps these women just happened to be standing near the camera.

I page through all the screens on the site, looking at dates for events in different cities which I will probably never travel to. I read the list of cities—Atlanta, Boston, Charlotte, Chicago, Dallas, Denver, and on through the alphabet, seventeen cities in all—as if trying to validate my participation in tonight's event by assuring myself that others have gone to similar events in lots of other places. People have posted testimonials, all enthusiastic and punctuated with exclamation points, to demonstrate how much fun the events are. "Amazing. I've never seen anything like it, all the gorgeous women of a popular club, but none of the noise, and with my key, I was able to approach, like, one hundred fifty different women to see if I unlocked."

I don't know what I'm searching for exactly. Something confirming I'll have a good time? Something telling me I won't feel like a fool for walking in the door? Whatever it is, it's not there on the Web site. What I am looking for is some evidence that I don't have to go to this event. Because I don't want to. I am intimidated by the idea of walking into a party by myself. Reverting back to my fears on the first day of seventh grade, I am worried everyone will turn and stare at me and label me a loser for coming to a singles party. I don't know what I think everyone else is doing there. I have to assume they're single and hoping to meet each other, too. But it doesn't matter. I am nervous. I am intimidated. The bottom line is that I don't care how easy the event organizers make it for me to start conversations with the men who attend. I don't care if I will get a built-in prop to talk about. I just don't want to go.

I have run headlong into a big reason why it's so hard to find dates in the twenty-first century. Sometimes we'd rather stay home than lean on awkward conventions to help us meet each other.

For many of us, standing around trying to make conversation for two hours at the end of a long work week is the last thing in the world we feel like doing. I calculate the hour I will have to leave work in order to fight traffic and arrive at the designated bar by 6:30 in time for check-in. I'll have to be out the door between 5:00 and 5:30. Few of us have jobs that actually end at that hour.

Plus, the clothes I'm wearing to work are not exactly the ideal wardrobe for a night of mingling in a hip bar. I'm wearing a white button-up shirt and a black skirt. Boring. I was too rushed in the morning to plan out the outfit I'd want to be wearing for trendy socializing at the end of the day. But traffic and wardrobe aside, I am just plain tired. I worked hard all week and the idea of pasting a smile on my face and forcing conversations just seems like more work. Therein lies another big problem with our social lives. Some of us are just too tired to date.

trying again

A couple weeks later, I go back to the Lock and Key party's Web site and find another event that's being held the following week. I boldly send in my RSVP, stopping short of actually paying in advance, because that would really mean I'm committing and that's a bold, scary thing. But at least I'm forcing myself one step closer to attending the next event, which will likely mean I'll go. Sure enough, a couple days later, I am skirting between the ropes outside a formerly hip bar and pool club in Santa Monica, California. I think it used to be owned by the pop icon Prince. Maybe it still is. All I know is I haven't set foot in the place in probably a decade, and I'm no cooler now than I was then. I take a quick look around before entering and breathe a sigh of relief: there is no flamboyant sign heralding this as a singles event. Until I get inside.

At the top of a dark, narrow stairway, I am greeted by one of the event's hosts, who plasters a name tag on my chest and hands me a small white card. There are instructions on one side and a flip side with three blank lines for contact information, should I meet someone I want to see again. And with it, a small red golf pencil with the event's trademark slogan: "Unlock your possibilities at the ultimate icebreaker party." It really is like seventh grade. I'm searching for my secret buddy.

Some of the instructions do not fill me with confidence. "Don't be shy. Women may approach men & vice versa." Sounds modern enough. "Please respect each other's space when trying." Now I am filled with fear. Am I going to be groped or held down while some man tries to open my lock? "If you don't unlock, you can talk a while or move on." This really is assisted socializing. What would the event be like if we didn't receive instructions?

There is already a crowd forming at the dark wood-paneled bar, where a bartender with a big smile pours apple martinis in front of a mirrored wall displaying backlit bottles of flavored vodka. People look a little too interested in the television which is soundlessly broadcasting a college basketball highlights show. The lighting is dim and the red sconces cast a sophisticated glow over the room, which is long and narrow with oversized leather booths along one wall and a row of bar stools on the other. It's 6:45, and we're told to sit tight and enjoy the free appetizers until 7:00 when the real excitement will begin: we'll line up to receive our locks and keys, and the madcap mingling will commence. I am too nervous to bother with appetizers so I just make my way toward the friendly bartender. He hands me my own fruity drink and I overtip him, subconsciously trying to buy an ally.

With drink in hand, I try to make eye contact with the other basketball watchers, figuring we're all here to socialize. If I get into a conversation, I can save myself the awkwardness of standing lamely at the bar, gazing at what is now a beer commercial. But it's like I'm a pariah, flouting Lock and Key etiquette by attempting to break the ice without my sexually suggestive prop. No one returns my gaze. No one talks to me. The crowd is mixed, ranging in age from early thirties to early fifties, in various ethnicities. Most people arrive in pairs of friends or small groups. No one looks especially cool at one extreme or socially inept at the other. Except for me. I am alone in a bar full of people, all of whom seem keenly aware of my misery. One guy even points me out to his friend. But his friend doesn't come over. He just laughs the laugh of someone who isn't standing at the bar of a singles event alone, nursing a cranberry drink.

I probably wouldn't be standing at a singles event at all (I'm married and generally avoid events which invite me to "unlock my possibilities"), but this is research. The only way I can objectively assess the state of dating today is to go undercover, as it were, and experience our methods and services firsthand. I have rules for myself in this undertaking: I will not lead anyone on, which means no actual dates; I will focus my research on the age group of nineteen- to forty-five-year-olds, who, numbering eighty-three million, are the target market of dating services; I will not lie or create an alter ego who would behave the way I *think* a single thirty-five-year-old would act; and finally, I will approach each dating experience with objectivity, but also with the hopefulness anyone brings to a first date. So when I attend the Lock and Key party, I'm hoping to discover an inside track to dating nirvana.

staring into my drink

Donald takes pity on me. Donald is a balding mustachioed man in his forties with a friendly smile. He's the same height as me.

"Have you done this before?" he asks.

"No," I tell him. "Have you?"

"No, never," Donald says. He tells me he just thought he'd give it a try with a couple of his buddies.

"It seems like a decent way to socialize," I say blandly, realizing the worst possible truth: I am really boring. I try to make conversation with Donald, and with each attempt to come up with something, anything, to talk about, my self-esteem plummets. I realize how bad I am at this. And worse, Donald realizes it, too. He looks off into the distance, like he's hoping something out there will give him an excuse to run away. Unfortunately for all of us who've ever gazed off that way, there never is.

Donald and I regress to the most banal of topics, the "Where are you from?" variety. It turns out Donald is from Wisconsin and is shocked beyond belief to find out that I am a native Californian. Now we've hit on something we can run with. "Wow, I've lived here for seven years and I almost never meet anyone who's actually from here," he says, in a refrain I've heard about as often as I've taken a shower. Finding something we can talk about seems to make Donald more comfortable. Comfortable enough to get honest.

"Actually, now that I think about it, I have been to one other Lock and Key party," he says, looking at the ceiling as though trying to figure out how it slipped his mind. "It was in another part of town, though. So that's probably why I didn't remember." Even in a room filled with people attending a singles event, we don't want to admit we're so hard up to meet people that we'd attend a singles event.

"Did you meet anyone?" I ask. Donald says he met three people at the other party, and one of them led to a date.

"Not bad odds, I'd say," he tells me. And then as if realizing that his odds will improve if he stops talking to me—or at least if he meets more people—he bluntly tells me he's going to move on. "But my friends and I are going to play pool after this is over, if you're interested," he says. It's a safe tack to take. If I like him, I can find him at the pool tables. And if I don't, he won't have embarrassed himself by asking for my number.

I retreat to the restroom. It feels like the only safe place in the joint, since I did not come with a passel of gal pals who I can stand and talk to until it's time to get my lock. Most of the people who are waiting in the bar are clustered into groups of friends and are not doing any outside socializing in advance of the prescribed time.

"Some of these girls are a little too eager to be here," says a voice from beneath one of the stalls in the restroom.

"Yeah," says her friend, one stall over. "I've just gotta put on a smile and pretend I paid for this for a reason."

"Well, if I get really irritated, I'll just go next door until it's all over," her friend says.

They emerge from their respective stalls and look at me sympathetically, as though we all share the same pain. And almost as if on cue, Robert, the Lock and Key host, chimes in on a micro-phone, telling the women to line up on the left, men on the right, so we can receive our locks and keys. We exit the restroom and queue up.

moo

Men and women shuffle forward in our respective lines, like cattle heading for slaughter, no one daring to crack a smile. At the front of the line, two women at a table return the smile-free counte-nance and solemnly hand me a lock on a neon pink string. I ex-amine it before slipping it over my head. It's a brass Brinks padlock, a high-security device with a few ounces of heft to attest to its purpose. My neck strains forward with the weight when I slip it on. I wonder if my socializing will feel different now. My lock is like a permission slip that allows me to approach anyone or be approached, fear-free. Will I suddenly find that the world of friendly conversation is open to me when it wasn't before?

Actually, no.

I walk back into the fray near the bar, which has become packed in the twenty minutes since I have arrived, and am imme-diately approached by a tall, serious man who says only, "May I?" He holds out his key and I proffer my lock. He inserts his key, gives it a hearty jiggle in both directions and admits defeat when the lock doesn't open. "Oh, well," he says and keeps right on walking to the next lock-wearing prospect. I am taken aback. Isn't the whole point of the lock-and-key props to give us an icebreaker so we can get into conversations with each other? "How about if I give you a try?" says a stout guy in his thirties with a shaved head. He inserts his key. "Nope. Darn," he says and moves on. I soon realize that our props are the only ones doing the meeting and greeting.

"Let me try," says a tall man with white hair. He gives the lock a jerk and a twist and tries to force it open with brute strength. "I really thought this was gonna be the one," he says. I try to waylay him to see if he might be interested in having a conversation. "Gotta keep moving if I'm going to find my match," he says, apologetically. I wonder if he believes in magic, the kind of true kismet that could lead him to a lock he can open and the potential love of his life. Or maybe he's just really eager to turn in his lock in exchange for raffle tickets.

I go back to the bar for another drink. "Hi," says Jim. He has dark hair and a ruddy complexion. "Have you had any luck with that thing?" he asks, pointing to my lock.

"No," I say.

"Did you come far for this event?" he wants to know. I tell him I live nearby, and he lets me know he came with a group of friends who live about an hour south of Los Angeles. We talk for a few minutes. The conversation is pleasant enough, but I'm antsy to get away. Even though I've been frustrated by the all-business nature of my lock-and-key encounters so far, I'm still not interested in spending a long time talking to Jim. He's way too eager, and he's giving off the vibe of someone who's just desperate to get into a conversation with someone, anyone. Kind of the way I was a half hour earlier. But now I have my lock. I tell Jim I'm going to mingle a little and see if I can get it opened. Jim proffers his key, as though in a last-ditch attempt to see if maybe we really are a match and I'm just too blind to see. The lock doesn't open. It gives me a different type of permission slip—the kind I need to leave.

"Should we see if we're a fit?" a young redheaded guy in a sport coat says when I turn away from the bar. I hold up my lock to make it easier for him to slip in his key. The sexual metaphor is lost on no one. "Ooh, it's a tight fit," he says. I am relieved when he extracts his key and moves on.

A tall blond man comes up to me and wordlessly grabs my lock and inserts his key, all the while looking off into the distance as he tries unsuccessfully to get it open. He moves on without ever making eye contact or saying a word. If the locks and keys are an apt metaphor for sex, this man is not doing much to further his cause.

Then I hear a jubilant cheer from a stout, bouncy woman in her early fifties, standing next to me, as she holds up her opened lock. "We did it," she says to the key-bearing guy in his early thirties who opened her lock. He looks equally pleased. They're a physical mismatch, easily a twenty-year age difference between them. She looks like she could be his mother. But they march off arm in arm to the table at the front to exchange their lock and key for a new set and a pair of raffle tickets.

forgettable encounters

After about forty minutes, everyone starts to get confused about whose locks or keys they've already tried. One guy turns away from the bar and looks at me. "Have I already done you?" he asks.

"I'm not sure," I say. He proffers his key, and my lock springs open. "I guess we haven't tried each other yet," he says, introducing himself as Jerry. We walk to the front and exchange our apparatus for a fresh set. "I came to one of these before and it was just like this," he says.

"Really? I'm surprised," I tell him. "People seem really focused on finding a match but I wonder if anyone is using the icebreaker as a chance to get to know each other." Maybe it's just me.

"I think everyone is just trying to collect raffle tickets. If they knew how bad the prizes are, they'd probably be just having conversations," Jerry says. He tells me he came with a bunch of friends just for fun. "It's something to do on a Saturday night. Plus, I'm kind of shy, so I'm not really good at meeting people," he adds.

None of us is. Even though we're primates just like the prairie voles that release hormones which encourage them to bond and care for their young, we are often at a loss. But it's not for lack of our own subtle cues, says Helen Fisher, anthropologist and author of *Why We Love*. "The first thing someone does is set up a territory and try to draw attention to themselves with the loud laugh, smiling, exaggerated body motions. Then, when you come within courting range, you start grooming talk, the voice is higher and smoother, and it's best to start with compliments or questions.

Then the pickup escalates when somebody touches." Is that the purpose of our clumsy props?

While we're talking, a man walks up to me and sticks out his key. "Can we?" he asks. His key is unsuccessful and he moves on. Jerry and I try to resume our somewhat boring conversation, and a woman comes up to him. "Excuse me," she says to me. And she holds out her lock. Jerry tries his key to no avail. I am surprised that the normal rules of social etiquette don't seem to apply here. If a man and a woman were having a conversation at a bar or a party, it would be rude and awkward for someone to cut in. But in this situation, etiquette flies out the window in favor of getting the job done. In this case, unlocking is the order of the day.

The room is packed with bodies pressed into one another, having loud conversations and testing the strength of Brinks security. I scan the room and try to assess whether anyone seems to have moved beyond the task of unlocking and into a substantive conversation. It's hard to tell. People are still doing a lot of mingling and testing out their locks and keys. I even notice Robert, the Lock and Key party host, walking through the crowd with his own key around his neck, joining in on the fun.

I wonder what we are all doing here. Maybe it's just a game. Maybe we're so estranged from normal human contact that we revert to the formality of utilitarian pursuits: we're here to open locks, so we'd better not let dating get in the way. Or maybe the locks and keys are too strong a crutch. They do the connecting so we don't have to. Can we stop unlocking long enough to see if there's anyone in the room we'd like to date?

Maybe there is. "I got two phone numbers," I overhear a woman say to her male friend, showing him the little white card with event instructions on one side and two phone numbers scrawled on the back. "Wow, I'm encouraged," her friend says. She gives him a thumbs-up and scurries off to talk to more people. So, it turns out, human contact *is* possible. Amid all the odd social etiquette and the single-minded pursuit of unlocking, people are, in fact, making connections that may lead to dates. As to the kismet in fitting a single lock and key together and finding romance, I may be expecting too much.

In this day of waning chaperon, it requires real dexterity to keep a man on the string and yet never let him get an opportunity to make a direct pass. Often you would like him as a beau, but not as a lover. If you ever give a man a chance to declare his intentions, honorable or otherwise, in words or by pantomime, your friendship is over and you have only two alternatives—to take him up on it or to refuse him. Of course a man will not go on forever in the role of potential lover, but if you are clever, you can gain time by seeing to it that he never has a real opportunity to explain his feelings.

FROM *No Nice Girl Swears*, ALICE-LEONE MOATS, 1933

2.

all's quiet in
new york

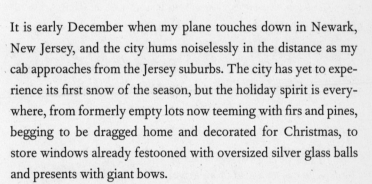

It is early December when my plane touches down in Newark, New Jersey, and the city hums noiselessly in the distance as my cab approaches from the Jersey suburbs. The city has yet to experience its first snow of the season, but the holiday spirit is everywhere, from formerly empty lots now teeming with firs and pines, begging to be dragged home and decorated for Christmas, to store windows already festooned with oversized silver glass balls and presents with giant bows.

The bar scene is alive and well in New York City, if for no other reason than due to the sheer volume of people who live and work in the city and who yearn to escape the restrictive walls of their homes. Pastis holds court in the meatpacking district, and its patrons spill out onto the sidewalk. The bar, which wraps around the center of the large open room, is packed three deep from end to end, bleeding into the restaurant's tables, where people might be able to dine in peace if not for the loud bark of conversations and the elbows of bar patrons edging into their plates of coq au vin.

It is impossible to stand at this bar and talk to no one, merely because of the forced proximity of the sixteen people pressing up against me from every direction. If I want to order a drink, I have to do it via one of five people between the bar and myself. Forget all the advice from dating experts—this is an instant icebreaker. And it leads to conversation.

"Why is it that all the women in New York wear black?" a guy named Sam asks me.

"I don't know if it's just New York," I tell him. "Black is just an easy choice. You don't have to think about it." This isn't to say that such a conversation would lead to a date. But it certainly comes naturally between two people who are mashed together in a bubbly atmosphere of postwork relaxation. Maybe the ubiquitous bar scene really is a good way to meet people. Sam cranes his neck over the three people between the bar and himself and puts in my drink order. "What is *pastis*, anyway?" he asks.

"It's French, made with aniseed. Tastes like licorice," I tell him, as he passes a wad of bills over the heads of other bar patrons and hands me a glass of the stuff. "Sounds awful. And pretentious," he says. And turns back toward his friends near the bar. Maybe it's not such a great way to meet people, after all.

dating obstacles

The next morning, it begins to snow—first in light flurries that flow horizontally past the window and aren't long for this world on the heavily trodden sidewalks, which just get very wet. I hop on the subway in SoHo and emerge ten minutes later in Midtown to find everything covered in white. And it keeps coming down, loading several inches on the tops of cars and garbage bags on the sidewalks in a matter of hours. The storm shows no signs of stopping, and the weather reports predict a foot or more by the next morning. And the entire dating scene in Manhattan is altered. It's more difficult to get a cab—nearly impossible, actually. The subways are packed and therefore much less pleasant a ride as wet cold bodies press into one another's coats and snowy scarves. Bars and restaurants are a welcome haven, though getting to them requires some extra motivation.

I walk toward Blaggard's, a neighborhood Irish pub somewhere between Times Square and Chelsea. This particular bar is hosting an event called a Quiet Party, which is popping up in a few cities across the United States as well as the seemingly random location of Beijing, China. The concept was borne out of necessity for those who find the typical bar scene fraught with dating obstacles, not the least of which is the often deafening volume of conversations, music, and martini shakers that makes an introductory chat a challenge at best, impossible at worst. At a Quiet Party, no one talks at all and the music is kept intentionally low. All interaction takes place on small index cards that can be passed like notes between a giggling schoolgirl and the boy who pulls her hair.

It takes the concept of looking good on paper to a new level: conversing well on paper. Plus, the added cuteness of sending a furtive note. It's not like the concept is new. Men and women for centuries have committed their most intimate thoughts to each other in letters. But generally it was because they had to rely on the Pony Express to connect them across vast distances before they had phones on which to talk to each other. We, on the other hand, are just looking for a placebo for live conversation, an excuse *not* to talk to each other.

I turn down a block in the mid-Forties and find that there's no one on the snowy street and no activity on the entire crosstown stretch, save the small lighted sign for Blaggard's. I push through the heavy wooden door, expecting a quiet scene of hushed voices and mad scribbling on paper. I imagine the cute intimacy of receiving a secret admirer's missive in a high school locker. Instead, I find a quiet scene of seven people and a bartender. Either the Quiet Party is a total bust, or I'm in the wrong place.

Instead, I learn that the party is postponed a week due to the blizzard. It turns out that in some cities, on some nights, dating is weather dependent. Even the most intrepid social butterflies will occasionally get stymied by snow or freezing rain. The seven people in the bar are the ones who, like me, either didn't check the Quiet Party Web site or didn't get the e-mail telling them the party had been canceled due to weather. So instead of passing notes, there are eight of us forced to make regular conversation.

"I come here when I want to hide out from my girlfriend," says Jeff, thirty-three, who lives down the block and is a regular. He knows all the bartenders by first name, and they know he likes to have a steady parade of Budweisers placed in front of him until he closes out his tab. Jeff proceeds to tell me about the relationship that's on the brink of collapse. He met his girlfriend, Katherine, thirty-one, when he was visiting his brother in Philadelphia, where he grew up. He went to a bar in Center City and ended up talking to Katherine for hours while he waited for his brother to show up. They dated long-distance for a few months until Jeff, a bond trader on Wall Street, asked her to move to New York. She quit her job waiting tables, moved in with Jeff, and now works in a retail store.

"She's so needy," Jeff says. "She's always going through these big emotional things and she just expects me to prop her up all the time. I don't even know what she's upset about," he says.

We talk some more. Jeff says Katherine is upset this evening because her family wanted her to fly to Kennebunkport in Maine for a social event. Jeff booked a flight, but because of the storm, they couldn't get off the ground. So he took her to dinner at an expensive steak restaurant instead, but not before he first invited a couple of friends from work to join them.

"That may be where you went wrong," I tell him. "She probably wanted to have a romantic dinner with you since your plans got canceled, and you went and invited other people along." I don't even know Katherine but from what Jeff has told me so far, this sounds about right.

"Yeah, she doesn't really like my friends from work," he admits. "That's probably why I invited them. Subconsciously." Jeff finishes the last of his beer. Another arrives on cue. "Thanks, Mike," he tells the bartender. Then he turns to me. "I know I'm not gonna marry this girl. I should break up with her. I can't marry a girl I don't love, right?"

"No, you probably shouldn't," I say.

"If I'm still dating her in six months, I'm gonna die."

waiting for someone to make a move

Amelia, thirty, sits on a bar stool with her friend, Jim, whom she "dragged" to the Quiet Party to keep her company. Jim, a former theater major who plans to go to graduate school in creative writing, feigns cynicism about going to a dating event. But Amelia chides him: "It's not like you're dating anyone."

I ask Amelia what appealed to her about the Quiet Party concept. "I hate coming to bars," she says. "I feel like guys need to take more initiative to ask women out. They need to take the lead. If they come to an event where they are forced to write things on paper, maybe they'll be more aggressive."

But beyond the romantic implications of passing a note, there is another level of comfort. For a generation that spends most of each day in front of a computer terminal, writing notes is the way we get things done. We've removed one level of contact by replacing conversations with notes, which can be read and reread at the recipient's convenience. And we've gotten comfortable communicating on paper. So even when faced with each other in person, there's a comfort level to writing things down.

Jim laughs at Amelia. "Why does it always have to be the guy who takes the lead?"

"Because when I ask a guy out, he thinks it means I'm in love with him," she says. "Guys say they want women to take the initiative, but then they get freaked out when we do. So what's the point?"

Jim tells her he'd love it if some woman asked him out. "But then again, I'm just here to keep you company. I'm not looking to date right now," he says. Jim is twenty-seven and has the air of an intellectual guy who acts confident right up until the time he has to make a romantic move. And Amelia knows he's full of it. "You so want to meet someone," she says. "You're just afraid of rejection."

"Who isn't?" Jim wants to know.

Amelia looks at me as if her point has been proved. "Maybe it's just the guys I know," Amelia says. "I went to Oberlin, so it was kind of an artsy place. The guys there were sensitive artistic types but they'd never make a move."

making the best of it

Gina doffs a red-and-white ski hat with a big fluffy ball on the end. She's dressed in black with fuzzy snow boots and already seems pretty drunk. She's a petite brunette with a big smile and has migrated from an animated conversation with the two guys at the end of the bar, to an intense talk with Jeff, to a conspiratorial chat with the bartender, which results in a cascade of disco music from the jukebox. He pours her another Jack and Coke, and Gina starts to dance. "Come on you guys, dance with me," she tells the rest of us. No one takes her up on it. She tries again: "Come on, I'm not hitting on any of you. You can dance with me."

Gina dances alone for a few minutes, lost in the music of her preteen years. She puts her red-and-white cap back on and spins around in circles. Then she bounces from person to person at the bar, giving each one a kiss on the cheek. "I'm so happy, I love this song." she says. "Jessie's Girl" by Rick Springfield pours from the jukebox.

Despite her blitzed goofiness, Gina is no dummy. She is a documentary producer with a two-year relationship in her recent past and is hoping to find a new romance. For her, the idea of writing notes instead of talking just seemed like proof that the people attending the event would have to be "at least a little bit intellectual," she says.

moving on

Jeff continues to drink his girlfriend into a distant memory, and Gina begs each of us to come with her to another bar she likes in Brooklyn. Amelia and Jim leave to go hear a band. Another group of intrepid drinkers takes up residence on the bar stools, and the bartender shuffles off to get their drinks. And onward with our lives. I leave Blaggard's and hop in a cab, in search of other bar scenes that promise to make dating easier. Farther downtown, I check out Remote Lounge, which has all kinds of contraptions designed to remove the awkward reality of meeting in person and replace it with the technology that is our comfort zone.

Remote Lounge is just like the legions of bars in New York or in any other city for that matter, save one striking difference: the tables have computer terminals and Web cameras on them. It's a gimmick, to be sure, but its popularity is evidence that we like gimmicks, or at the very least, that we just like anything new. The idea of Remote Lounge is simple. Bar patrons can behave like we normally would, standing and drinking together and venturing over to speak to one another if interested. Or we can behave like the technology fiends we are. We can study the computer terminals in front of us and watch what the men and women around us are doing. If we spot someone particularly appealing, we can dash off an introductory message.

Remote Lounge provides yet another opportunity to erect a barrier between ourselves and the people we hope to meet. It is almost as though we yearn for the days of an appointed chaperone to play interference. We are removing ourselves from firsthand contact and using the comfortable familiarity of technology to pave the way toward an eventual conversation. But despite the convenience and the novelty of the Webcams, they don't seem to be improving my ability to socialize in Remote Lounge. They are more of a neat party trick, a way to entertain myself while I sit at a table. It's momentarily amusing to watch three guys talking and pointing at their camera a few tables away. But I do not feel inclined to type them a message. And they appear to feel the same. After an hour, my computer terminal sits blank. It's late. I walk home.

coffee dates

The next morning, my quest for enhanced dating opportunities in the bar and coffeehouse scene takes me to Drip Café, a small sparse coffee shop on the upper West Side. The café distinguishes itself from the other caffeine fuel stations in the city in that this one is replete with books of profiles of single men and women. While drinking a small café au lait, I'm told, I can look through the books and choose someone I'd like to date. The staff of Drip Café will then make contact for me and arrange a date, which will take place either at Drip itself or at one of several bars around the city that are affiliated with Drip. There is something vaguely academic about sitting in a booth, shopping for dates, as it were.

The Drip concept sounds simple enough. I take the subway to the upper West Side and slog through about a foot of snow that has piled up on the sidewalk, only to find that Drip is closed for renovation. There is a sign directing me to check its Web site for dating opportunities. I log on and find that the Drip offerings are not so different from those on any number of online dating sites. Men and women list their basic physical attributes, religious affiliation, turn-ons and turnoffs.

John, a profile that matches my search criteria, lists himself as six feet tall, spiritual, bald or shaved head, and a consultant by occupation. His interests are dancing, fitness, reading, and sports, and he says that looks shouldn't matter but they do. On the surface, he matches many of the people I'm friends with and would probably be a perfectly nice date. But I do not need to arrange a coffee date at Drip Café if I am interested in meeting someone on the Web. There are dozens of online dating services designed just for that purpose.

I am zero for three in New York.

In a city of three million single adults, the bar scene is not a lock for dating success. Even with added gimmicks to facilitate socializing, we're still left to our own humble devices, which, often as not, don't serve us too well. It is not only in New York City that the low-tech dating landscape has spawned creative interpretations. Single residents of Amarillo, Texas, can go to a "roundup" hosted by the Texas Association of Single Square Dancers, and concepts like "Eight on a Date" or "Table for Six" pair up men and women for dinner parties in cities across the country. And intrepid New Yorkers can attend a "Dinner in the Dark," where they dine on tactile foods and get to know one another in complete blackness, only to put a face to the conversation at the end of the meal.

In Paris, supermarket dating is the next new thing. Lafayette Gourmet, which runs the food hall at the Galeries Lafayette shopping center, has turned Thursday nights into a dating-while-shopping opportunity, in which single shoppers use special purple shopping carts with a kissing couple on the front. To make the mingling more productive—or at least to lower inhibitions about discussing the merits of various cheeses—single shoppers get champagne and a free photo if they succeed at making conversation with a potential match. To me it feels like pressure to dispense with dandruff shampoo and dried prunes in favor of exotic olives and wine. I like to shop under the radar, so low-tech or not, supermarket dating does not appeal. I need to delve deeper. Maybe the answer lies in speed.

part two

speed and efficiency

Janel, thirty-five, is very open to meeting new people. If she's sitting next to someone single at a dinner party, she'll make friendly conversation. "I decided I have to aggressively tell my friends I want them to introduce me to people or I'm going to be single forever," says Janel, an African-American woman from Atlanta. But even the blind dates that go well don't turn into relationships. "He'll say to my friend, 'I never thought you would introduce me to someone so fantastic. This is the kind of girl you'd marry, and I'm not really ready for that so I can't date her,'" she says. Janel, an executive at a film company, has heard it over and over again to the point where she just assumes it is true for new men she meets. "I need someone who is on top of his game, who isn't going to feel intimidated by my career success," she says. "I shouldn't have to apologize for it."

Two years of bad blind dates have led Janel to seek out other avenues—namely, a high-end dating service that caters to successful professionals. She makes her way to a gray glass office building next to a fancy Chinese restaurant in Beverly Hills. There are Persian rugs on the floors and sample books filled with the kinds of men they promise Janel will meet through their service. From the moment she arrives, she is skeptical that the dating service is the right answer for her, even though a friend of hers successfully met her husband that way. "I just got a weird feeling about the place," Janel says. "Part of it comes from the idea of paying for dates."

For a single fee of $6,000, the dating service promises to find seven good prospects. "I sat down and they showed me samples of the kind of men they could match me with. They all seemed legitimately interesting," Janel says. "Then they left me alone in the room for a few minutes to think about it." As Janel glances through the books of prospective dates, she notices a sign advertising another dating service run by the same company. This one boasts men who will pay $20,000 to meet models. "It sounded like an escort service," Janel says. She's immediately wary and asks if that part of the company is legitimate. The company assures her that it is. "I said, 'Well, do the women pay, too?'" It turns out that the company's other dating service requires only the men to pay. "I said, 'That sounds like prostitution to me,' and asked for my forms back and left."

Fed up with contrivances, Janel is hoping to meet someone on a plane or through a friend. Otherwise it just seems like too much work. "All the time I was growing up, my mom instilled good work values. But recently I said to her, 'Why didn't you tell me I needed to spend my time working to meet a man?'" Janel says. "I feel like I'm being punished for being successful. It fosters bitterness. Every guy who says, 'She's really great—I can't call her' is a slap in the face to everything you've become."

Love and sex are nature's salesmen, and she works them overtime to draw the victim into investing before he even has time to think things out . . . Men like lovemaking, but don't give them too much of it! Small tidbits of love served nicely are like those highly flavored canapés; something to smack the lips over and remember with pleasure, but you don't want too many of them or you sicken for life.

FROM *Live with a Man and Love It,* BY ANNE FISHER, 1937

3.

the dating agent

♥

♥

♥

At age twenty-six, Robert has about a year to go before he's considered over the hill. In a twist on the traditional biological clock, Robert is abiding by a religious clock, one set by Orthodox Judaism. In the religious community, and according to the mores of certain cultures, the mandate is to marry young and have large families. "After about age twenty-seven, religious people start wondering what's wrong with you," Robert says. But he's lucky on one count: he's male. "Women need to be married by age twenty-four at the absolute latest or they are considered no good anymore," he says.

Age requirements are not the only obstacle. Searching for a woman with similar Orthodox values is a challenge in Toronto, where Robert has lived for three years. Or, for that matter, in Vancouver, where he lived before that. "I knew I was in trouble when the only person who was like me in terms of religiosity was the rabbi's wife. And she was already taken," Robert says. He had used the Internet to meet people with similar values but never really called on it to find dates. Instead he's opted for the more traditional route and employed a *shadchan*, or matchmaker. "I don't meet Jewish girls anywhere," he says. "It's not appropriate to go up to a girl in the grocery store and ask her out so there are not many options for meeting people with a similar degree of religiosity."

Robert was not always religiously devout. Raised by a doctor and a journalist in a moderately religious household, Robert became interested in Orthodox values during college, when he spent a year away from the Christian university he was attending and went to Hebrew University in Israel. During the rest of college and law school, Robert kept Shabbat, not answering the phone on Friday nights, spending Saturdays in a synagogue, dating only Jewish women, and vowing that he'll be respectful and serious about them. Robert realizes he doesn't know many Orthodox Jewish women and that he lacks a real network for meeting them. He's aware that if he wants to meet Jewish women who share his values, he'll have to move to a different city and hire a matchmaker, formally known as a *shadchan*.

I can relate. After striking out at socializing opportunities on both coasts, I'm ready to see if more personalized matchmaking holds the key to dating success.

it's just a phone call

I intentionally wait until after 6:00 P.M. to call the dating service "It's Just Lunch!," hoping to get an answering machine. Not that I want to leave a message. I just want to hear the outgoing greeting and gather whatever information is available before the beep. It's part of my dating recon, like dipping a toe in to test the waters before talking to a real person. But I'm in no such luck. A real person answers the phone at 6:45 and I'm plunged into the deep end.

"What brings you to us today?" asks the woman on the other end of the line.

"I was just thinking about using a dating service, so I wanted to get some information," I tell her. "Sure, hang on one minute," she tells me, no doubt running to another room to say she's got a live one on the line.

Dorothy picks up the phone. She has a zealous, tinkling voice and wants to know how I heard about "It's Just Lunch!" I tell her I know someone who used the service. I say it's hard to meet people because I have a demanding job. I tell her I've been on plenty of blind dates, but now I'm looking for better odds. I'm hoping that a dating service operated by "professionals" will have more successful methods of matching me up. "It will be a totally different experience," Dorothy assures me.

Dorothy tells me that most of her clients are referrals, just like me. "They're tired of fix-ups," Dorothy says. "They're professional people who don't want to date their clients," she says. Just like me. I wonder if I'd told Dorothy that I'd seen the company's ad in a newspaper and that I'd tried Internet dating, if she would have told me most of her clients matched those characteristics, too. I'm supposed to feel at home, but I can't tell if I'm being played.

"I have a thousand clients," Dorothy says, reading me their statistics: 95 percent have college degrees, 70 percent have advanced degrees. "They are entertainment people, doctors, lawyers, bankers," she says. "We pick an equidistant restaurant to both of your workplaces and arrange a lunch date or an after-work cocktail for you. I tell you what he looks like and why I think you'll be a good match," she says. After the lunch date, I'll report back to Dorothy and let her know if she was right. A brochure from "It's Just Lunch!" cites that 86 percent of singles prefer lunch or drinks after work for a first date, and Dorothy is following the rule of thumb.

Formal Orthodox matchmakers like the one Robert uses take their jobs very seriously. And they get paid, either in cash or gifts. Some are paid only if the couple ends up getting married—$500 or more—and others are paid per session. "It's Just Lunch!" which says it has twenty-five thousand members in more than fifty cities, charges $1,500 for fourteen dates or a year of matchmaking. Dorothy will meet with me for an hour and glean enough crucial information about my likes and dislikes to make educated choices about which clients to match with me. I wonder how that's possible. For years, some of my closest friends made valiant efforts to set me up on blind dates with coworkers they knew well or friends who had a lot in common with me. And most of those were a bust. "It's Just Lunch!" says there is a 17 percent chance of liking a date set up by a friend, according to a survey of three thousand of their clients. But I wonder about the odds of liking someone Dorothy selects.

I ask Dorothy why her dating service is better than just having my friends set me up. If I'm spending more than $100 per date, I want to be sure Dorothy has much better skill than the friends who know me well.

Dorothy again references her one thousand clients, which give her a lot more choices than my friends might have. But it's hard to get past the fact that Dorothy can only figure out so much about me in a forty-five-minute interview. "A lot of it's trial and error," Dorothy says. "I'll send you out on the first date, and when I get your feedback, I'll know whether I'm choosing the right types for you."

We talk some more. Dorothy says our meeting will help her learn about my definition of attractive. "We'll talk about what went wrong in your past relationships. But don't bring any pictures of your exes!" she twitters. "That's a no-no."

Ultimately, Dorothy is a salesperson, not unlike the telemarketers who call me after dinner and hope to keep talking long enough to wheedle a donation out of me before I can make an excuse and hang up. Dorothy's goal is to reel me in for an in-person meeting, which is one step away from having me invest in her services. I agree to set up a meeting, but warn her that my schedule is busy until the following week.

"I'd really hate to have you wait that long," Dorothy says. "I could get you started tomorrow if you could just find the time." For the average person who, to begin with, has probably hemmed and hawed for weeks before calling a dating service, another week is not a big deal. But I sense the urgency: if I don't commit to a meeting now, Dorothy might lose her chance. It's Wednesday and she tells me she can fit me in first thing on Friday. I tell her I'll check my schedule and if it doesn't work, we can plan for the following week.

The next day, I get an annoyed-sounding voice-mail message from Dorothy. "Well, I haven't heard from you, so, um, I guess I should just schedule someone else in your slot? I have someone who's waiting for my call, but the slot is yours if you want it, so let me know." I start to get cold feet. Day after tomorrow feels too soon. Next week feels safer. While I'm debating what to do, I get another voice-mail message: "It's me again and you haven't called me back. I don't know what to think. I guess you're not interested." *Click.*

I wonder if the passive-aggressive tone works on her other clients. Am I supposed to feel guilty for not getting back to her right away? Should I be worrying that I have a narrow window of opportunity with Dorothy and her dating service that will slam shut forever if I don't clear my schedule?

love me, love my matchmaker

Finding a good matchmaker, it turns out, is almost as hard as finding a good match.

"I get in fights with my *shadchan* sometimes," Robert says. He relies on her to do formal background checks on women who might be a good match and to call their references before suggesting a date, but their tastes don't always match up. "My *shadchan* suggested a girl and I asked for a description and she said, 'She's the kind of girl who goes to synagogue on Friday nights,'" Robert says. "I figure that's a code for the fact that she weighs three hundred eighty-five pounds." Robert isn't interested in dating women whom he doesn't connect with initially. And that includes physical appearance. His *shadchan* tells him love is supposed to grow. She worries that he has a mistaken set of values. She feels distraught. Robert decides they need some time apart.

His next *shadchan* seems to understand his needs a bit better. "She does her research and will send me better prospects," Robert says. She also screens potential blind dates whom friends offer to set him up with. "I use her as my agent. If someone wants to set me up, I say, 'Call Mavi.' If she doesn't think the girl measures up, she'll nix her for me." The *shadchan* functions as more than just an introduction service. She acts as a go-between in Robert's relationships with women he's dating. Sort of the dating-related version of "have my people call your people." If he dates someone he's not interested in going out with again, he doesn't have to make the awkward phone call to say so. His *shadchan* lets Robert's date know he's not interested in seeing her again.

Orthodox matchmakers also function as relationship therapists, helping a couple work out early issues. "A friend of mine went out with a girl and thought she wore too much makeup. He told the *shadchan*, and she had a talk with the girl," Robert says. "The next time they went out, she wore less makeup, and he was attracted to her. Now they're married." It's common in the Orthodox community to date for two or three months before getting married. Robert says he'll probably break with tradition and date for a longer period of time, but he has to find someone first.

As I replay Dorothy's messages on my answering machine, I contemplate my own set of options. I can use a different matchmaker or even a service called TheraDate, in which therapists use extensive questionnaires to match clients with complementary personalities. And neuroses. I imagine the personal statement: "SWM in therapy for slight obsessive-compulsive tendencies seeking SF in therapy for something interesting but treatable. Must be nonsmoker willing to share the bed with my three cats. In return I will rearrange your condiments several times a day and cook you vegan alternative meals."

Or I can give Dorothy a chance. The thought of another awkward introductory phone call makes Dorothy seem like my dearest friend and hard-won confidante. And besides, dating itself is based on the premise of giving someone a chance, even when we have virtually nothing to go on. So I ignore Dorothy's off-putting messages and call her to schedule an appointment for the following week.

Dorothy leaves me a bright, enthusiastic voice-mail message with directions. "Bring yourself, your day-planner, and a checkbook, 'cause we don't take credit cards."

it's just an interview

There's always a foreboding feeling that comes with walking through the door to meet a person with the potential to change your life forever. It's the same feeling I get when I walk into a gym I'm thinking of joining. I know the salespeople have been primed: "Don't let her out the door without getting a commitment of two years." "Flatter her, then tell her all the success stories of people more out of shape than her who now look like goddesses thanks to our personal trainers—who, incidentally, cost extra."

I've heard the pitches. I know the pitches. Even if the result is a dream relationship or the perfect figure, stepping through the portal is scary. But more frightening, and more realistic, is the possibility that stepping through the door of a dating service or any other business will lead to us mortgaging our homes before we know it and signing up for a lifetime membership that will yield no real results at all. As a stopgap, I intentionally leave my checkbook at home.

I walk down the hall of a large office high-rise, looking for the door to dating nirvana. It's locked. I ring a bell. A delivery man comes down the hallway toward me. Is he giving me a knowing smirk? I stare at the floor until he passes. The door opens and a perky, young woman named Donna welcomes me. The office is a tiny room with a side table loaded with brochures, and four doors, all of them closed. In her phone call, Dorothy had professed absolute confidentiality and had guaranteed that I wouldn't share the waiting room with any other clients. "Like when you go to the shrink," she tells me, laughing, as though she's certain we share the bond of therapy.

Donna ushers me immediately into a small room and hands me some paperwork to fill out before closing the door. The room is white with two purple "accent walls," adorned with framed newspaper and magazine articles going back ten years about the company and its founder. A small gray table is loaded with brochures and photocopies of more news articles about the dating service and its success. I look over two pages of questions attached to a clipboard. It's the standard fare about what I'm looking for in a date or mate: age range, degree of attractiveness, smoking habits, level of education, children. Then there's a page listing activities: bowling, cooking, photography, hiking, running, skiing, reading, dining, entertaining. The list goes on. I'm instructed to circle the activities I like best.

My initial instinct is to indicate that religion isn't that important, that looks don't matter, and that I'm not concerned about education level. I want to appear easygoing. But it quickly dawns on me that if a dating service is charging $1,500 to find prospective matches, I should shoot for the moon. If we lie and say none of those things matter, we might as well let some stranger on the street find us dates. The whole point of paying a dating service, it seems, is to get what we want. So I get specific. He has to be Jewish. My desired age range is thirty to forty. Looks *are* important.

It takes me about three minutes to fill out the forms, so I'm left with a good five to ten minutes until Dorothy comes into the room. I don't know if this lag time is intentional or if Dorothy is busy with someone else. Or maybe she didn't expect me to blitz through the list of questions with time to spare. But the time is not welcome. I don't want to read the company's promotional materials, even though the company's founder did meet her own husband when he came through the door as a prospective client. I just want to get on with it.

Dorothy knocks on the door and comes in to shake my hand. I put her age at midthirties to early forties. She has long, sandy-blond hair and plain features and wears an electric blue wraparound dress and strappy sandals. It's the middle of winter and

I'm distracted by her pale legs, crossed as she sits in the chair opposite me. We get down to business.

Dorothy looks over my forms, uttering a few "hmms" just like my doctor does when she reviews my chart. Then she starts in with a list of questions. How often do you work out? How important is physical fitness? What were the good and bad qualities in your prior relationships? What are the deal breakers, the qualities you could never live with under any circumstances?

I do my best to answer. "I can't handle someone who hates his job but is doing nothing to change the situation. I'd need to be with someone who knows what he wants to do with his life and is doing it," I tell her.

"So you want someone who has a career, not a job," Dorothy says, reducing my description to a truism.

"How important is a man's physique?" she asks, explaining that a lot of her male clients are really into their workouts and specify that they only want to date women who are in great shape. I tell her I'm a runner and have been one for years.

"So you'd say you're into working out? It's not just something you do, but more a part of your life?" she asks, with some agenda she doesn't explain.

Then she wants to know my bare minimums. Height parameters, big turnoffs, the importance of looks. I want to tell her I'm not that picky, but let's face it, we're all picky. And it doesn't do anyone any good to pretend we have lax standards when we only get a fixed number of dates for our payment. It seems like we're paying for access to people we aren't going to find in the course of our daily lives. It begins to feel like buying a car, where we have the ability to specify the options we want. If we're paying top dollar, should we expect our dates to come fully loaded?

"Does a man have to be tall or is it okay if he's slight or short?" Dorothy wants to know. I tell her it's not a big turn-on if a guy is small. No woman wants to spend the night and borrow a pair of boxer shorts, only to find that they're too tiny. Dorothy laughs and chirps at my answers to her questions. It's almost like she's trying to date me, like she wants to make me feel flattered by her interest and encourage me to keep talking.

I don't give Dorothy much to go on. Some of my answers to her questions are intentionally vague. Yes, I like to dance. Yes, I like to go to parties. I say I'm drawn to creative people. I tell her it's a pet peeve when a man doesn't read a newspaper and has no interest in what's going on in the world. But still, these are random slices of what's important to me. It's not clear how Dorothy can glean enough in forty-five minutes to figure out whom I'd really get along with.

the sales pitch

Dorothy and I run through the get-to-know-you portion of our meeting, and she inhales deeply before presenting me with the big pitch. "I can already think of a few men I can't wait for you to meet. I'm really so excited about this," she says. I wonder if she ever says anything different to anyone else. "So when do you want to get started?" she asks. I demur. I'm not sure it feels comfortable. In all honesty, has she made me feel confident in her matching abilities? Or am I just supposed to trust her?

"I'm ready to get moving today. I could have you dating by this weekend," she says. Again, it doesn't exactly feel scientific. Sure, Dorothy could pluck one of the five-hundred-odd clients she has and send me out with him, but is she merely taking shots and hoping for the best? Or is there something her years of training allows her to see in me that will yield an accurate match?

I tell Dorothy I'm not ready to take the plunge. I tell her I'm still not convinced that she can offer me such different results than friends who will set up blind dates for free. "Your friends don't have five hundred people to choose from," Dorothy says, arguing her case. But I'm not sure quantity equals quality. Just because Dorothy has files to dig through, it doesn't mean she will have better luck than anyone else. And for $1,500, I expect more of a guarantee.

Dorothy is reluctant to let me leave without committing to becoming a client. She dismisses my concerns about the likelihood of a match. "Yeah, it's rolling the dice," Dorothy admits. "But at least it's rolling the dice with people who cared enough to plunk down $1,500." I'm not sure mutual willingness to pay money guarantees compatibility. She wheedles a bit more. "I could have you dating by the weekend. Don't you want to get out there?" I tell her I'll think about it and be in touch.

Dorothy leaves me with a final plea. "Look, if I find you a date, I'm not saying it will be a match, but I promise that you'll have a good time." And as though she senses she's losing the battle, Dorothy summons the company mantra, telling me, "It's just lunch."

meet me at the waldorf

Out of the blue Robert gets a call from a matchmaker in Israel who got his name from one of the rabbis of a congregation where Robert used to be a member. She interviews him thoroughly, asking how much time he spends studying the Torah, what his values are, how observant he is of religious customs. She decides that Robert meets her criteria and tells him she wants to introduce him to a woman who lives in New York City, even though he lives several hundred miles away. A month later, Robert is visiting a friend in New York, so he tells the matchmaker he's ready to meet his prospective date, whose name is Rachel. Rachel's father wants to speak to Robert before the date is set up.

"I'm thinking this is a little weird but I decide I'll be a good sport and go along with it," Robert says. He answers his phone.

It is the father, speaking in a heavy accent: "You are religious?" he asks.

"Yes," Robert says.

"You wear *kippah*? You learn Torah?"

"Yes, I do," Robert says, wondering what he's gotten himself into.

"You keep Shabbat?" he asks. "You are a lawyer?"

"Yes," says Robert.

"Good. I have a suite at Waldorf Astoria Hotel. You meet me there," Rachel's father says. And hangs up.

Robert is not sure whether to meet him or not. "I'm thinking this is totally ludicrous, but I decide to do it, anyway," he says. Robert goes to the hotel and waits in the lobby. He sees a man walk up with a woman and a girl behind him. They sit. "I'm thinking, 'Crap, I'm on a date with a girl and her parents.'"

Robert looks at Rachel. "She was a knockout. And I don't want the father to beat me for staring at his daughter." Rachel's father begins asking Robert a slew of questions about where he was raised, what kind of law he practices. All the while, he does not introduce his wife or Rachel to Robert. After about an hour of screening, Rachel's father takes his wife by the arm and leaves to go shopping, so Rachel and Robert can have twenty minutes alone together. "I'm thinking she's nice, but there's no way I'm getting involved in this."

The parents return, and Robert tries to make conversations with Rachel's mother. She won't engage, doesn't seem interested in talking to Robert. "It becomes clear to me that her mother doesn't like me."

After the date, Robert calls Rachel's father to thank him. But there will be no second date. According to a survey by "It's Just Lunch!" for 79 percent of men, it takes fifteen minutes on a first date to decide whether to go out on a second.

phone sales

The day after we meet, Dorothy calls to tell me she already has a few ideas for me. She's eager to tell me about the men she could set me up with and says she can send a courier over for a check and have me dating by the weekend.

First, there's Lyle, a forty-one-year-old professional musician who describes himself as lean and fit. Lyle likes to read and considers himself a social person who enjoys parties and dinners in restaurants. "He's looking for someone who's into growth, continual growth," Dorothy tells me. "We described him as warm, empathetic, in good shape, and adorable."

Dorothy's other pick is Bob, a thirty-four-year-old optometrist who went to grad school and is a nonpracticing Catholic. "We describe him as a good provider, sweet, and looking for his partner in crime," Dorothy says. She reads his list of interests: dining, fitness, golf, suspense novels, politics, basketball, social drinking, and travel. "He's communicative, someone who can really draw people out but a little shy and easygoing," Dorothy says.

It's hard to know if I'd have anything to say to these men if I met them in person. But of the five-hundred-odd men Dorothy has as clients, it seems strange that the two she chose for me do not meet the basic requirements I listed on the information sheet I filled out for her. Lyle is forty-one, just outside my thirty- to forty-age range, and Bob is not Jewish. I am not impressed with the vast assortment of choices Dorothy advertises, given that she can't stay within my most basic parameters.

Dorothy leaves me another message. "I'm calling to get feedback on my choices for you," she says. "I'm wondering if you've made any decisions or if you're still apprehensive. I just have a feeling that apprehension may be there until we push you out there on a first date."

Before I get a chance to check my messages, Dorothy calls again. "I may be driving you crazy, but I'm just really excited about these matches for you," she says. I find it odd that she's so excited about setting me up with men whom she describes in rather generic terms. Granted, she has matched up our interests, but she's still falling short on the basic request that a potential date fall within a ten-year age range and that he be Jewish.

I call Dorothy back and tell her I don't think she and I are seeing eye to eye. She emphasizes that none of these dates have to lead to a serious relationship. "It's just a date. It's just for fun," she says, pleading with me to let her fix me up. "But that's the reason I feel like we're not on the same page," I tell her. "I don't want just another date. I want to think you're selecting people who I'd really have a chance of connecting with." Isn't that the point?

The next day, Dorothy leaves another message. "I just want to thank you for opening my eyes to something. I've been doing this for seven years and no one has ever told me we weren't seeing eye to eye, so I just wanted to thank you," she says, obliquely. Is it one last-ditch effort to manipulate me into signing up with the service? Dorothy says she'll keep my data in her files and talks through the information she's gleaned from our meeting. "I have you down as someone who wants a partner who is on the path they've chosen. I like your comment that you try on a guy's underwear and don't like it when it's too tight. I've written down that you're tired of the B.S. and you're looking for someone who is topical and knows current events." Do I really come across as a news junkie with an underwear fetish?

I listen to her prattle on about my characteristics and can understand why she chose the men she did. She gleaned that I'm fixated on tiny underpants and chose tall, well-built men. She picked men who read and like politics. And she topped it off with a helping of generic adjectives. Dorothy leaves me with a final thought: "Maybe I did get an accurate picture of you, after all. So maybe you'll let me help you get out there and have some fun."

I stop and consider whether I am giving "It's Just Lunch!" fair consideration. Does the fact that I am not really looking for a date afford me the right to be cynical? After all, the company boasts ten thousand marriages have resulted from successful matchmaking in its twelve-year history. So clearly the form of matchmaking Dorothy offers can be successful. Maybe it has something to do with the motivation of two people who've paid $1,500 in hope of finding love. But paying someone to act as a matchmaker automatically raises expectations. It only makes sense to pay money for something if we're truly getting a service we can't provide for ourselves. And what of the hundreds of thousands of lunch dates set up by "It's Just Lunch!" that didn't lead to a wedding toast? We simply don't hear about them. It's not good business. I decide to move on.

in toronto

Weeks go by and Robert's *shadchan* has not produced results. He is starting to get impatient, realizing he won't look like such a good prospect in another couple of years. Then he gets a call from a rabbi he knows, telling him about a woman named Ariel he might be interested in dating. He refers the call to his *shadchan*, who had coincidentally just heard about Ariel from another source. Robert's *shadchan* does her research and background checks and decides Ariel is a good match for Robert. They set up a time to meet.

"She's great," Robert says, sounding uplifted for the first time since we've spoken. He goes out with her for his requisite one or two dates and is still interested. They continue dating. For a month. It's the longest relationship Robert has had with a woman he met through his matchmaker. "I'm optimistic," he says. "Maybe this time things will work out."

Two months go by, and Ariel goes to Israel for eight weeks. She and Robert keep in touch. "I was more religious than she was so I wondered if she'd be more in the same place when she came back," Robert says. "And she was."

They date four more months, which is starting to skim the outer edges of acceptability in the Orthodox community. There is no physical intimacy in Orthodox relationships before marriage, so by those standards it was feeling long as well. Then Robert asks Ariel's parents' permission to get engaged. Ariel and her parents accept.

Robert buys his *shadchan* a nice vase as a thank-you gift. Ariel does the same for her *shadchan*. Now they are on their own. They plan for a four-month engagement, also considered a bit long by Orthodox standards. But from first date until wedding day, their relationship is under a year. "Love is supposed to grow. The majority develops after marriage," Robert says. "If you have the same morals and values and have fun, the thought is, Let's get the show on the road."

When one of the "stags" standing in the doorway sees a girl dance past whom he wants to dance with, he darts forward, lays his hand on the shoulder of her partner, who relinquishes his place in favor of the newcomer, and a third in turn does the same to him. Or, the one who was first dancing with her, may "cut in on" the partner who took her from him, after she has danced once around the ballroom. This seemingly far from polite maneuver, is considered correct behavior in best society in Boston, New York, Philadelphia, Buffalo, Pittsburgh, Chicago, San Francisco, and therefore most likely in all parts of America.

FROM *Etiquette: The Blue Book of Social Usage,*
BY EMILY POST, 1922

4.

dating at warp speed—
my evening with
HurryDate

♥

♥

♥

I pull open the heavy wood door at the Westwood Brewing Company and take a quick scan around the room. I wonder if the people I see talking animatedly at the Los Angeles bar are there for the speed-dating event that is supposed to take place in twenty minutes. Like any bar scene, this one is marked by the sweeping swivel of heads that turn each time the front door opens, as if people are awaiting the arrival of someone they know. But they aren't awaiting the arrival of anyone. It's just ingrained bar behavior, the neck crane and head corkscrew to see if the new person walking through the door is *someone*.

Not only am I not someone, I am slightly embarrassed to be

entering the bar at all. I wonder if the patrons who have swiveled around to stare briefly can tell that I'm there to speed-date. I wonder if I have the equivalent of a sign on my forehead that labels me the kind of desperate, dateless sap who would go to a singles event. Or maybe they merely think I'm the kind of desperate dateless sap who goes to bars alone, hoping to meet someone, or that I've been stood up by the people I'm supposed to meet there. Most likely they're not thinking anything. They're just looking at me the same way they're looking at everyone who walks through the door, as though we need to prove we're worthy of their company.

I don't see any signs or hoopla celebrating an evening of speed-dating and fear that I may be in the wrong place. I think about asking at the hostess desk where the event is being held, but I am not ready yet to admit that level of desperation: not only am I so inept at finding men that I need to attend a mixer, I am also so inept that I need help finding the mixer.

But after walking from one end of the bar to the other two times, I see nothing resembling an event. It must be upstairs. But I can't find the stairs. Maybe I *am* that inept. "How do I get upstairs?" I ask the hostess, determined not to say the word "dating" or "singles."

"Oh, for the speed-dating?" she asks, taking what is clear pleasure in saying the name. She points me back through the bar, out to a patio staircase, which I reach only after passing every possible bar patron one more time.

At the top of the stairs, I see that I am not alone. Two women I'd seen in the parking lot are checking in and sticking small squares of paper on their sweaters. An event that requires name tags.

my compatriots

"Oh, you're doing this, too," one of the women from the parking lot says when she notices me standing next to them. She's written her name in block letters on her name tag: KIM. Her friend seems to be resisting, putting the sticker in her pocket instead.

"She made me do it," the friend says, pointing to Kim, a broadly smiling, tiny brunette wearing all black.

"I figured, how bad can it be, right?" Kim says.

"Right," Kim's friend says, rolling her eyes as if to say that it could, in fact, be pretty bad. Few of us are big fans of contrived situations where we're supposed to meet people, whether they are for career networking or forced socializing. Probably for this reason, many of the people at this event are in the company of a friend. It provides a safe fallback option in case the evening is a total bust, ensuring there's at least one person in the room they're willing to talk to.

Kim and her friend look me over. There's a lot of sizing up going on in these first few minutes. Everyone is wondering who actually goes to a speed-dating event. Do we look normal? Are we losers?

Both of them tell me this is their first time trying speed-dating. That turns out to be true of most people at this event. Most of them say that a friend of theirs tried speed-dating in another city and recommended it. Most also say they can't believe they're doing this. Everyone feels a need to explain why they're here, even though we're all here for the same reason.

HurryDate, the company hosting the event, promises an

evening of twenty-five dates for three minutes apiece. If any two people indicate they'd like to see each other again, they are considered a "match" and they receive each other's e-mail addresses afterward so they can set up a real date sometime in the future. For all this serendipity, HurryDate charges $35 and promises "drink specials."

When I check in, I am given a name tag, a pen, a scorecard, and a number. I am Fifteen.

The idea is that each time I talk to a guy, he will make a mental note of my number and use it to indicate whether he'd like to go out with me again. He too will have his name and a number written on his name tag, and I will circle a "yes" or a "no" on my scorecard to indicate whether I'd like to see him again. In order to avoid leading anyone on, I plan to circle "no" for everyone. I feel a little guilty about wasting their time and handing out needless rejection, but I take comfort in the fact that they will be meeting twenty-four other women who may choose to date them again. Plus, I remind myself, most of us are quite picky when it comes to a romantic match. I'm probably not the only one who will end up circling all "noes."

I should state for the record that I am breaking no rules. Nowhere in the terms of participation does it require me to state whether or not I am single. This turns out to be true for all of the dating events and services I investigate. Maybe it's just assumed that we're all single, or maybe it doesn't matter.

Different companies and social groups offer variations on the speed-dating theme. The first speed-dating event was an offshoot of a networking group for Jewish singles. They allowed participants to meet seven others for seven minutes apiece. Not surprisingly, dozens of speed-dating outfits have sprung up all over the nation. There is speed-dating over billiards, speed-dating for the career minded, for athletic singles. And speed-dating events have expanded in age range, branching out from the twenty-five to thirty-five-year-old mainstay. But essentially they provide the same service: mass introductions in minimal time.

speed-dating for boomers

Across town, Carlos Pianelli is getting ready for his own speed-dating event. Carlos was once a single guy who was in search of a speed-dating event to jump-start his romantic life. Today he is a single guy who runs Fast Track Romance in Los Angeles in the hope of jump-starting other people's romantic lives. "I'm looking at it from a romantic point of view," says Carlos, who teaches middle school and started Fast Track after going to another company's speed-dating event and deciding he could do better. "Singles love romance. So we hold our events in a restaurant, so it feels like a date." Carlos also chooses to hold events on Sunday nights so no one has to fight traffic. Mindy opts to attend such an event, held at a restaurant in a boat-filled marina on a Sunday night at five o'clock. She is unforgiving of the crowd, which is in the thirty-five- to fifty-age range.

"This is a fuddy-duddy crowd. There are two guys with gray hair," she says, pointing to two men who are dressed in khaki pants and blue denim shirts. "I'm at a fuddy-duddy age," says Mindy, who is forty-two. "Even if the guys are my age, they look like that. Somehow I've reached the age when people who I can go out with are either much older or they are younger but they look older. They're the ones who are available." But Mindy has resigned herself to giving speed-dating a try. "I don't meet anyone by sitting at home. And I really doubt I'll meet anyone here. But at least this gets me out so I can feel like I'm participating," she says.

Andy is thirty-eight and wears his heart on his sleeve. "I'm despondent," he tells Mindy, adding that he hasn't met anyone he wants to date in the six years since he moved to Los Angeles. "It's hard to meet people. I work alone on a computer every day." Andy sells motorcycle accessories to racing enthusiasts from his home computer. "I'm thinking about joining a gym to try and meet people," he says. "Right now I'm into motorcycle racing, but I don't meet a lot of women that way." Andy turns to a balding man holding a martini and begins telling him the same story.

Mindy takes a cursory look around the bar and sizes up the other people there for the event. She shakes her head. No one interests her. And she's relieved. "I would be more scared if there was someone here who I thought I would want to go out with," she says. "Then I'm opening myself up to failure. This way, I can just look at it as an experience."

hurry up and date

I choose HurryDate because it seems to be fairly representative of the speed-dating events that occur every week all over the country. This one has the added bonus of being somewhat close to where I live. So it's decided. I will meet two dozen people and watch them cycle past me like leaves in a hurricane.

I take a quick glance around the room. With still a full fifteen minutes before the HurryDating is supposed to begin, people are milling around, ordering drinks at the bar, glancing furtively at their watches. A few have already seated themselves at the small tables where the hurried dating will take place. I head for the bar.

The bar provides a sense of purpose and an excuse for standing around, waiting. I make a big production of scanning the different bottles of beer that are displayed on a countertop below a row of taps. I finally order a Guinness and find myself face-to-goatee with a guy who is downing the last of something that looks like cider.

We make small talk, and I realize that I have inadvertently wandered into an old-fashioned bar scene. After we get through the "Have you ever done this before?" conversation, we launch into regular bar small talk. I remark that this event seems like sorority rush, where college women are paraded through sorority houses and rated, "carried," or rejected based on short superficial conversations.

"Oh, were you in a sorority?" he wants to know. I guess I asked for it.

We manage to get through the next fifteen minutes, talking about how crowded the bar seems to be getting and staring way too long at a muted television that is broadcasting sports highlights. I am relieved at 7:30 when our excruciating spell of small talk is over, until I realize that sometime in the next hour and a half we will be paired up to chat for three minutes more.

on your marks, get set

We are told to begin taking our seats. The room conjures memories of taking the SATs at small desks lined up in a room. There is no ambient lighting, just the harsh glare of overhead houselights. There are tables for four arranged along one wall under a bank of open windows, a handful of round tables in the middle of the room, and another row of tables along the opposite brick wall. Each table is labeled with a letter of the alphabet from A to Y, twenty-five in all. The women are told to sit on one side of the tables. The men are told to sit across from us, and they begin finding seats until the room is buzzing with fifty people chattering and looking around in nervous anticipation like kids at a camp sing-along. I sit in front of the letter Y.

Three more people sit and we smile at one another awkwardly and pretend to read the instructions on our scorecards, even though most of us know exactly what we're supposed to be doing. There are "prompter" questions on a half sheet of paper on each table. In case we can't come up with enough things to talk about, we are being given some fallback conversation starters. The topics range from the insipid to the intrusive. What is your favorite ice-cream flavor? How do you like to be kissed? Do you have an archenemy? Do you believe in ghosts? Have you ever stolen anything? Would you like to be famous? Have you ever had your heart broken? Can you roll your tongue?

"Oh, God," says the woman seated to my right when she reads the conversation topics. "Favorite ice-cream flavor? That's something you get to way later in a relationship. I don't need to know that now."

"I like the one about the archenemy," I say. The other three at my table look at me like I've just announced I ate nine kittens on my way over to the bar. I realize I'm already moving toward alienating everyone at my table. I backtrack.

"I'm not saying I have a lot of archenemies or anything. I'm thinking of it more like anyone or anything that gets you riled up. I'd be interested in knowing that about a person." They still look suspicious but decide to let it go. I vow to keep the rest of my opinions to myself. I also pray that none of the guys I'm about to meet plans on asking me if I've ever had my heart broken or if there's a special way I like to be kissed. Way too personal, way too soon, and not exactly the kind of thing I like to talk about with complete strangers. Even if we are linked by the common bond of having come to this event together.

"I just hope they're coming around to take drink orders. There's no way I can do this on only one drink," says the woman to my right, whose name turns out to be Sherrie. "You're brave," she says to Victor, one of the two guys at our table. "You're doing this without drinking at all?"

"Well, I was told there would be no bathroom breaks. I don't want to miss out on talking to the woman of my dreams because I have to wee-wee," he says.

introductions all around

I look around the wood-paneled room from one anxious face to another and wonder if anyone here is going to meet a true romantic match in the next hour.

"How about we each say why we're here," Sherrie suggests. "I'd be interested in knowing what brought everyone to this event." I look at her sideways. Is she gathering material like I am? I want to know why everyone is here, too, but I was planning on being much less direct in finding out.

"My friend dragged me with him," says Tom, pointing to someone sitting at the next table. "I don't go to bars or anything. It's so uncomfortable just standing there, trying to meet people. But this seemed like a good way to meet a lot of people."

Tom is right. It does feel awkward to stand in a bar, trying to meet people. We are long past the era of arranged marriages and have full freedom to choose our own dates. This freedom is hard-won, and it is the envy of young men and women who live in cultures today where religious and social strictures insist on arranged relationships. And we've never been more at a loss for how to find the great loves of our lives. Is speed-dating the answer?

"What about you?" I ask Victor, who's sitting across from me.

"It seemed very efficient. The time aspect appealed to me, the idea of investing minimal time to meet a bunch of people. It's a dollar and forty cents a person," he says, referring to the $35 fee to meet twenty-five people in one evening. I guess it was inevitable that someone would break down the concept into economic terms.

Sherrie takes her turn. "I was never into the bar scene, either.

I don't really go out much so it's hard to meet people. So we came together," she says, pointing to her friend at the table next to ours.

These three are a pretty fair representation of the whole. Nobody stands out as a social deviant, a shut-in, or an obnoxious swinger. It is a room full of people like any room full of people at a party, in a bar, or at a dot-com company picnic. There is racial diversity, a specified age range of twenty-five to thirty-five, and a general attitude of semi-disbelief that each of us ended up here.

I don't know what I expected—some subsection of the L.A. trendy singles scene or a sad bunch of losers on parade? Not exactly. Being single is not a disease. If anything, it is usually a sign of high standards and a relentless lifestyle that leave little time to meet people just in passing. We're not spending hours and hours of free time socializing in speakeasies. The coffee we drink, even in the vente latte size, gets splashed into a to-go cup and taken on the run. And we don't have community dances or big parties where the fox-trot would allow couples to mix and mingle on the dance floor according to a universally understood set of steps. The idea of being passed from one person to the next at a bar is not so different from square dancing with different partners throughout an evening, hoping to catch someone's eye. But somehow it still seems clumsier.

we sprint from the starting gates

Finally, our evening's host goes to a microphone and begins to explain the rules. Her name is Beckie and she is dressed in all black with a whistle and stopwatch each on a string around her neck.

"When I blow the whistle, you'll have three minutes to talk to the person sitting across from you. At the end of that time, indicate on your scorecard whether you'd like to continue your conversation with that person at a later date. Then the men will move one seat to their right, and you'll get another three minutes to talk to the next person. Ladies, stay seated the whole time."

Easy enough. The whistle blows.

I start talking to Victor, who has been sitting across from me for at least fifteen minutes already. We've been through the gamut of small talk, and I'm pretty sure he's as sick of me as I am of him, especially since he suspects me of having an inordinate number of enemies. Now, what are we supposed to talk about? A minute or so in, we realize we both like to travel.

"I've been everywhere except South America," he says.

"What do you have against South America?" I ask.

"Nothing. I'll probably go sometime soon."

"Do you have one place that you like that you go to over and over? Like mine is Paris. Whenever I fly somewhere, I try to go through Paris first," I tell him.

"Oh, Paris is your hub? Mine, too." So it turns out we have something in common after all. I start to get excited about talking about the places he's been and to trading travel stories. The whistle blows. Right in the middle of Victor's story about getting marooned in Venice during a rail strike. We shrug as if to say, "Oh, well," and he moves on.

Tom slides into the seat in front of me. "So where are you from?" he asks, immediately taking me back to every awkward blind date I've ever been on, thanks to my well-intentioned, though delusional and apparently myopic friends. The "Where are you from?" question turns out to be a popular opener at this event. I guess it is a harmless way to start a conversation and to find out a little about someone, but to me it reeks of handing someone your résumé. The only thing worse is asking, "So, what do you do?"

"So what do you do?" asks Paul, the next guy in the rotation after Tom. We talk about Paul's marketing job and the online educational business he's hoping to start one day. Paul is from Dallas but he doesn't have much of an accent. He seems surprised when I tell him this. I realize that he might in fact have an accent but it is so loud in the room of twenty-five urgent conversations that I would scarcely have known if Paul were acting out his conversation in pantomime. I glance around at the room full of guys I will need to talk to before I can go home. It is overwhelming.

sunset in the marina

Meanwhile, across town at the Fast Track event, Mindy meets a string of men. "Darryl was very nervous. His friend was supposed to meet him at the event and he didn't show up," Mindy says. Darryl's friend had talked him into coming to a speed-dating event in the first place, and Darryl, a blond-haired architect in his late forties, had called him from the car on his way over and offered to pick him up. His friend said he'd just meet him there but never showed up. "Instead of talking about ourselves, our conversation focused on Darryl and his frustration with trying to meet people. I felt like a therapist," Mindy says.

The pressure to make quick yet lasting impressions naturally breeds insecurity. "One man kept asking me how he was doing, whether he was giving me the right information, what else I wanted to know," Mindy says. It's natural to feel a panicked sense that we're not making the most of our allotted time. What if Carlos rings the bell before we've properly waxed poetic on some crucial topic we cannot possibly fit into a sound bite?

After meeting a few more men, Mindy decides to take on the therapist role in earnest. She sits with Andy who tells her he doesn't understand why he keeps getting rejected when he approaches women he finds attractive and asks them out. He tells Mindy a story about the last woman he liked. She worked for the United Parcel Service and when she helped Andy mail a package, he thought they had a rapport. So he UPS'ed her a rose the next day. "I said, 'You have to stop asking out anyone you see who is attractive. You have to stop scaring off women,'" Mindy says. "I think it's great that he has such a romantic gesture in mind but he's using it on the wrong people. He sees someone he likes and just blurts out that he wants to go out with them," Mindy says. "Not that I have the answers, either. If I'm supposed to end up with someone, it's not clear to me how I'm going to find him.

"The last guy I talked to was painful," Mindy continues. "He told me, 'I'm a thrill seeker, I like thrill seeking. I like scuba diving and motorcycles and rock climbing.' The whole time, his head was bobbing back and forth." Mindy tells him she's not interested in rock climbing or motorcycles but that sometimes people can have separate but complementary interests and still have a lot in common. He disagrees. "He said he doesn't believe that. He's looking for someone who wants to scuba dive and rock climb. I told him I'm not that person," Mindy says.

one hundred eighty seconds, one-twentieth of an hour

Beckie's whistle blows. Charles asks me what I like to do for fun, when I'm not working. I blather on about hiking and biking and generally doing things outdoors. Charles doesn't say much. He just looks at me when I'm finished speaking, as though I'm holding out on him and he's going to sit tight for more information. In reality, I think he's just all out of things to say. It is too soon in our relationship for long silences. I struggle to come up with filler.

"So, have you ever done this before?" I ask.

"No. You?"

"No."

Three minutes can be a very long time.

By about my sixth conversation, my brain starts to ache. I feel like I'm cramming for a test, like I've just read a hundred pages of notes in the minutes before the exam is about to start. How am I supposed to remember anything?

At this point in the evening, mass confusion is setting in. People are realizing that they are not meeting each other in numerical order. Most of the men say they've been circling "yesses" and "noes" beginning at number one, even though they've talked to a handful of us in no particular order. I realize I haven't even noticed the numbers on anyone's name tag.

Now each new conversation begins with a handshake and a careful look at the number on the name tag of the new person sitting across from each of us. In my case, each new conversation begins a slow descent into hell. What made me think my brain could handle this much gyration at the end of a long day? I find myself looking up occasionally at Beckie with the whistle to make sure she hasn't fallen asleep on the job. She appears to be minding her stopwatch, but I have my doubts.

Sam sits down. Sam has a way of looking straight at me with big owlish eyes that make me feel like he is trying to delve into my soul. "What are you looking for in a relationship?" he wants to know. It is one of those too personal and definitely way too deep questions to consider in a three-minute conversation. But I try my best to give him an honest answer.

"To me the best relationship is one where you feel like you have a real partner in crime, someone who you can talk to for hours about nothing really, someone you can travel with, someone you have a connection to." The whole time I'm talking, he is looking at me with those zombie eyes, like he's trying to decide if my response is earnest enough. I turn the tables. "What about you? What are you looking for?"

"Oh, someone I can do fun things with. Someone who likes to go out and do fun things," he says. I am so glad I bared my soul for "fun things." Beckie snaps out of what seems like a fifteen-minute stupor and blows the whistle.

And so it goes. I meet a biostatistician, a couple of engineers, a doctor, a cartoonist, and a guy who started a business to put ads on the sides of trucks. I meet men from cities across the United States, Canada, and Europe. We spend a lot of time talking about where we're from and what we do. I guess that's the currency we trade in at a time when our lives revolve around our jobs, and most of us live far from where we grew up.

I talk to Bruce, a blond composer who tells me all about his job. It's like he's auditioning for a new gig. I want to shake his hand at the end of the interview and tell him he sounds very qualified and that I'll keep him in mind should I have anything that needs musical accompaniment.

When John moves to the empty chair in front of me, he tells me he's a composer, too, preempting my reaction by adding that he and Bruce and the next guy in line are all composers and all friends. "You should know that, in case you want to go out with all of us, we'll probably talk about you." I can't imagine why someone would pass up the chance to be talked about. The third composer seems relieved that John has paved the way for him. We are free to talk about other things like what the three of them do when they're not composing and how the three of them know one another. It turns out they live together, too.

The whistle blows.

People have different approaches to these abbreviated conversations. Some speak in sound bites and lob rapid-fire questions, trying to get as much information as possible into the time allowed. Others seem to have a stock opening line of the "Where are you from?" variety and have nothing else prepared for backup. These conversations have big lags, where both of us look around the room and make observations about the fine grain of the varnished wood table where we sit.

I imagine that this type of socializing is not so different from the kind of arranged waltzes in the Victorian era, during which time men and women were passed from one to another at a dance given by a relative or a community group. But somehow the waltz conjures up a much more elegant set of rules and gestures. There is curtsying involved in the waltz, for one thing. And the pace of a dance is not rushed. There is the rhythm of the music to use as a guide, and certainly not a whistle to signal a change of partners.

But in some ways, speed-dating may just be the waltz of a generation with attention-deficit disorder. If the moves appear less graceful, it is only because we have ceased to consider grace to be a value worth pursuing. We've traded gowns flowing for whistles blowing. Speed is the name of the game.

round and round we go

Gary sits. Gary is the first guy so far who seems a bit socially awkward. He looks goofy and a little forlorn and he, too, asks me what I am looking for in a guy. Before I give him an abbreviated version of my soul mate/travel partner speech, I quickly turn the tables and ask what he's looking for. In three minutes maybe we'll never get to what I'm looking for.

"I'm looking for someone who is interested in me, who is interested in going out with me and getting to know me. I'm looking for a girl who doesn't play games. I hate games and I don't want to play any games. I want to go out with someone who likes me and who's honest." I wonder if this is where I'm supposed to tell him that I am that girl.

Gary has a printed spreadsheet with numbers and lines on it. He's taken a lot of notes on each woman he's met. I tell him I'm envious that he has a sheet like that because I'm already having trouble remembering who I've talked with.

"I made this sheet. I brought it with me after I did this one other time. I even gave a copy to my friend over there," he says.

I tell him that the sheet is a great idea and that I'm sure it helps. The whistle blows, and I am granted a reprieve from Gary and his sheet.

I talk with a string of computer scientists, one of whom is very insistent on knowing what kind of writing I do. By now I have gotten a bit better at timing the three-minute time span and have gained a feeling of control. I deftly deflect the conversation and before I know it, he is already two seats away. This way I am not forced to lie about who I am, what I'm doing there, and what I do for a living. Most of the time we never get into details, and I can deftly punt to a new topic. The men seem relieved when I do this because they are absolved of responsibility for thinking of what to say.

The whistle blows. A conversation ensues. Whistle. Conversation. Whistle. Whistle.

Speed-dating is the natural outgrowth of a culture with increasingly short attention spans. We have honed our dating radar to the point of being able to evaluate a relationship's potential in three minutes or less. We may be overlooking the great loves that grow with time, the people who are gun-shy and awkward in a stressful three-minute race-to-inform. But we are willing to live with that because we simply don't have the time to wait it out. Though maybe we should.

It makes me wonder what the next incarnation of speed-dating will look like. Will there be events with thirty-second introductions to two hundred people? Maybe the events will take place on conveyor belts, so valuable time won't be wasted moving from seat to seat.

There is another factor at work: the concept of maximum return from minimal investment. We're using economic principles here, principles normally devoted to the stock market or gaming tables. We don't want to throw good money after bad, or in dating terms, good quality time at poor quality romantic candidates, once we've decided there is no potential. So if a decision can be made over coffee, why risk having to sit through a three-course dinner? And if a decision can be made in three minutes, why invest five?

more spreadsheets

By this time in the evening, everyone is on information overload. As the men change seats after each whistle toot, there is leftover business from the previous person. Before any new introductions can take place, there is a lot of frantic note taking and scorecard shuffling. We've all realized that the only way to keep anyone straight is to write something down.

A guy named Guy bumps his way over to the seat across from me. He has the same spreadsheet as Gary, and I tell him I could use one right about now. I've been scribbling notes surreptitiously in the margins of my scorecard as the men change seats but there isn't much time. I don't know how anyone could manage to provide a handshake good-bye, make a few notes on a conversation's high points, circle "yes" or "no," and move seats in a matter of instants. That could take three minutes alone. But Guy seems to have his system down pat. "That's why I made this sheet."

"But I thought the other guy I talked to said he made the sheet," I say.

"He's lying. I made it. Here, I'll even prove it. I have extras." He shows me his stash of extra copies. I realize I have stumbled into a bizarre one-upmanship over who is more anal retentive.

"I've done this four times. Did the other guy tell you that, too? Because he's only done it twice." I try to deflect the conversation from what is becoming a heated battle. I remark that Guy must have had fun the last three times if he's back for more. He tells me that he's gotten a few dates but that he hasn't met the right woman yet. "I want to meet her by the end of the year. I have to. With the holidays coming and New Year's, I want to have someone." It is the middle of December. Guy does not seem concerned. "I've met some great women here tonight," he says. The mercy whistle blows.

The pace of meeting and greeting begins to wear on me. Just when I begin to hit a groove with someone, to leave behind the strains of small talk, and to hit on a subject that interests us both, the whistle sends him onward and brings me another man, another conversation, another set of biographical data. Name, handshake, basic exchange of information, awkward pauses, something interesting, whistle, good-bye. Name, handshake, basic exchange of information, and so on.

It is human channel surfing.

are we done yet? not even close

I meet Todd, a genetics professor from Germany. I tell him I just met another guy from Germany, just three or four seats ahead of him. He becomes intensely interested in craning his neck around to find his compatriot, and I do my best to point him out amid the tables. Truthfully, however, I don't even remember which one he is. That is the problem with oversupply. There's no way to distinguish one face from another, and I've met the men in such rapid-fire succession that my powers of recall are shot.

The whistle blows. Brian sits down. He's the only guy I've talked to so far who is wearing a business suit, making me aware for the first time that either today's workplaces have all truly shifted to business casual or that most men went home and changed. Brian looks at me and unleashes what I am certain is a prepared speech, possibly one he's been using on all the women there: "I knew this would happen. Right in the middle of the night I'd find myself talking to a pretty girl and I'd find myself tongue-tied and babbling—see, I'm doing it now. But hopefully you'll find that endearing."

I tell him that babbling is not a problem.

He continues: "Why don't we recap some of the conversations we've had so far? One of the women before you asked what brought me here tonight and I said, 'a Camry.'"

"Do you really have a Camry or were you just being funny?" I ask, hoping for the latter.

"Yep, I really have one. It's black."

It turns out that Brian is from Los Angeles, giving us something in common, though it does not exactly strike me as mind-scrambling kismet. Before we can go too far expressing our wonderment that two people from Los Angeles are actually sitting in the same room together, Beckie blows the whistle.

Next sits Dan, a doctor who tells me I look familiar. This is my greatest fear, that I will run into someone I know distantly. Any-

one I know well will understand that my dating spree is for research. But someone I barely know who recognizes me could
draw some incorrect conclusions without my realizing he is even
in the room. My initial scan of the crowd has given me some peace
of mind that I'm safe from running into anyone, but Dan has me
nervous. "Maybe we met at a Jewish singles event. Have you gone
to any of the Aish events?" he asks. I know Aish to be the Aish
HaTorah group which hosts mixers for Jewish singles. I tell Dan I
have never been to one. He says he doesn't believe me. I spend the
remaining minute and forty seconds trying to convince him.

Derrick sits down, still finishing his conversation with the
woman next to me, who is reminding him that she is "the fun one
who likes shopping." Our conversation begins where theirs apparently left off—with shopping. Derrick tells me he's not into
shopping. "I shop once a year and buy a bunch of suits and that's
it for another year. I wear a lot of Hugo Boss."

"Do you have a job where you have to wear suits to work?" I
ask, noticing that he's wearing a dark blue dress shirt, unbuttoned
at the top without a tie, and a tan suit jacket. I assume it's Hugo Boss.

"Actually, I don't. I can wear pretty much whatever I want to
work. I don't know why I buy so many suits. I really don't need to,"
he says, and he begins to look distressed. I am not sure how to console him. I tell him it's nice to wear suits to work, that it draws a
professional boundary. He doesn't seem at all convinced. "Really.
Now that I think about it, I have no reason to have so many suits."
Somehow our mindless conversation has brought on an existential
crisis. When our three minutes are up, I wish him luck as he rede-
fines himself through a new wardrobe and watch him shaking his
head as he moves on to the next unsuspecting woman.

Two minutes and forty seconds seems to be the magical time when small talk yields to a comfort level between two strangers. It makes me wonder if we would hit that same comfort zone fifty minutes into an hour or on the third date out of four if we allowed the time. Does speed-dating just rush our normal reactions because our time is limited? Or does the electronic age rush our reactions to everything, whether it's the decision to buy a stereo based on a thirty-second commercial or the option to send an instant message because e-mail is too slow?

how to lose your mind in an hour or less

My head begins to ache from the beer I drank over an hour ago, the forced get-to-know-you smile I've had plastered on my face for eighteen meetings or more, and the decibel level in a room where twenty-five pressing conversations are taking place at once.

Do I even remember the first guy I talked to? I try to remember that first conversation. It was something about travel, I think. And somewhere in there was a guy who was looking for a girl who was interested in dating him. There were three composers and two German guys. They have become interchangeable in my mind.

I'm experiencing this night in dog years. I wonder, if someone were doing this for real, how it would be possible to decide whom to consider dating again. If, for example, HurryDate sent me an e-mail saying that guys named Jim, Paul, and Ivan had circled "yes" for me and I them, would I even recognize one of them if he came to my door?

All the same, I can't say this is the worst way in the world to meet people. It's a bit contrived, but it does force people to talk to one another in an equal-opportunity way. That doesn't always happen at parties or other venues where there's dating potential.

The bottom line, however, is that a three-minute conversation is scarcely better than viewing someone's photo and biographical statement on a dating Web site. It provides only cursory information and only the most remote inkling whether there is any romantic future possible. The proof must ultimately be in a good old-fashioned date, whether over dinner or otherwise. We can make meeting people faster or more convenient, but we can still only get to know each other in real time.

I notice Victor, the first guy I talked to, moving along the row toward me. There's only one guy to his right, which means my twenty-five-person conversation binge is about to end. I am in no mood to start another conversation and I say as much to Steve, who sits across from me.

"Okay, I'm going to write 'No fun' next to your name," he says. I see that he has made a little list of all twenty-five women he's met so far and next to my name he writes, "No fun."

"I might be fun if I wasn't completely fried," I explain.

"No, that's okay. Don't worry about it. You're the last one. I'm sure you're fun." I realize it doesn't matter whether Steve thinks I'm fun or not. Chances are I'll never see Steve again. And maybe he decides the same is true for me, because we have the first relaxed, normal conversation I've had all evening. We laugh. We talk about nothing in particular. I start to feel myself re-humanizing.

The whistle ends the marathon. We're encouraged to vacate the tables so another round of speed-dating can begin. Beckie says there is room in round two for a few women and a few men to stay from the first group. I can't conceive of doing this again in five minutes. I see Guy, the one who wants to meet a woman by the end of the year, approach Beckie and offer to stay for the next round.

the recap

"Are you going to stay?" Sherrie asks me as we get up from our table.

"Nope, I've had enough," I tell her. "Talking with fifty guys in one night would probably break me."

"Oh, come on. Are you sure? We're gonna stay," she says, as her friend comes over.

"I can't do it. I'm beat," I say. I look around the room. No one is lining up to stay for round two. People are filing out, looking a bit dazed. Some have reunited with the friends they came with and are heading downstairs to the bar for a drink. But no one seems to be picking up on conversations they began in the three-minute speed round. Why risk rejection now, when a promised e-mail will arrive in a couple of days to affirm who was actually interested? Give us a crutch—we'll take it.

"Did you meet anyone good?" asks Sherrie's friend, whose name is Nina.

"There were some nice guys," Sherrie says.

"Oh, give me a break. I circled only three yesses and I was being nice. There was that guy with the muscles and that other one who was a doctor. But seriously, I didn't meet anyone I really want to go out with," Nina says.

"Of course you picked the guy with the muscles," Sherrie says. "You're so into that. So, really, you're only saying yes to three? What about you?" she asks me.

I shrug, leaving its meaning open to interpretation.

"Wow. I said yes to a lot. Like probably half," Sherrie says. "I thought a lot of them were nice." Nina leaves to tell Beckie that she and Sherrie will stay for the next round. "I thought this was really fun," Sherrie says. "I came from a small town where everyone was the same. Tonight I got to meet Asian guys and Jewish guys—people I wouldn't meet otherwise."

Sherrie is looking at her scorecard, which I can see has a lot of yesses. "I don't care what Nina says," she adds. "I'm going to keep all of these. So you're really not going to stay with us?" she asks. I stop and think. If I was really single and looking for love, would I stay for round two? Is my complacency born of exhaustion or lack of need?

It takes but a few seconds to make the distinction. I look at the bleary eyes of my fellow speed-daters from round one and realize I'm not alone. Twenty-five dates in less than two hours borders on overload, no matter how much we're hoping for romance. "No, I can't do it. Sorry. But have fun."

Nina comes back. She and Sherrie get busy comparing their scorecards, and I head for the exit. The next group of speed-daters filters in from the bar and begins to mill toward their seats.

As I turn in my scorecard, I notice some of the men I've met hunched over tables, looking at their notes and circling their choices.

I walk down the stairs and back through the bar, watching the heads swivel again in hope of seeing *someone*. I wonder how many of them have had meaningful conversations, whether three-minute or longer. I have my doubts.

For her part, Mindy hasn't had much luck at the Fast Track event, but she's not surprised. "I'm not going to go out with anyone here. I have no desire," she says. Mindy decides she's not interested in friendships, either. "There's one guy who is a stunt man who might be okay as a friend but he's good-looking and attractive. I'm sure he has lots of friends," she says. "People are here to see who else is like them, to reassure themselves they're normal, that they're okay." Mindy doesn't mark anyone down on her scorecard.

Carlos walks around and hands out raffle tickets and reads off the numbers of the winners. Mindy wins first prize, a thirty-day membership to a gym. Craig wins second prize, admission to a free Fast Track event. "This is fast-food dating. It's a numbers game. You have to put enough people in a room together to improve the odds," Carlos says.

For Andy, far from despondent, the odds may be turning. He lingers after the event, talking to a slight, curly-haired woman whom he met in the seven-minute session just beforehand. They look into each other's eyes, lean forward into their conversation, and tune out the rest of the people in the room. It's like a real date. Maybe it will lead to one.

responses at the speed
of snail mail

The next step for me is to go home and wait for HurryDate to send an e-mail revealing if any of us mutually selected each other when it came time to check our yes/no boxes. After the whirlwind chatting session, I sort of expect the response to come at light speed as well. It almost seems as if the e-mail should be waiting for me when I get home that night, even though I know it's not possible for the scorecards to be processed that fast.

I check the next morning, thinking I will have some perfunctory mass e-mail thanking me for participating and letting me know I will receive my results shortly. But there is nothing.

I look again the next morning, thinking surely one day is enough time to process the "yes" and "no" responses and notify us of how it went. But still no messages in my in-box. I'm not expecting to match with anyone but I do expect to receive my e-mail in which the dating service says it regrets to inform me that I received no matches from my evening of speed-dating. I'm curious to see whether they will offer me condolences for the fact that I am still dateless or perhaps advice about being less picky in the future.

I imagine that anyone who is hoping that future dates are in the works would be frustrated at having to wait several days to find out the results. It seems like a hiccup in the continuum of time to go from getting to know people in three minutes to waiting three days to know if there is hope of a future—that is, if an e-mail actually arrived on the third day.

The e-mail arrives on the fourth day. I am anxious to see how HurryDate will console me, since I am certain to have no matches. I wonder if they have a gently worded, kind response that will tell me that it's nothing personal, that some of the most wonderful, talented, attractive, lovely people sometimes find themselves without a match.

There is no such consolation. After an introductory paragraph in which HurryDate says its representatives hope I had a good time, I am told to look for my matches below. "If you don't have any matches listed, don't sweat it. It takes two to make a match. There are lots more HurryDaters waiting to meet you next time!" There is my consolation: if no one I selected chooses me as someone he'd like to date, I can always come back for more potential humiliation and strike out again and again. It doesn't quite seem comforting enough.

Then, the bad news: "Sorry, no matches were made. We hope to see you again. . . ." Even though I know the reins were clearly in my hands, those words still sting a bit. I imagine how those words would feel for those who really thought they had made a match that night. No one wants to be told they were a speed-dating casualty.

HurryDate's Web site asserts that for every one hundred men and women who meet on a given evening, there are usually 140 matches, meaning that some people probably get more than one, while others may get none at all. On average, however, those odds appear to be a dating success story.

And therein lies the harsh reality of speed-dating or any dating for that matter. Whether it's a failed attempt to make small talk with one person at a party or with two dozen people at warp speed, rejection hurts. Rejection by twenty-five people in a single evening has to feel that much worse than a single failure to get someone's phone number, even if the reality is that you were extra picky. Suddenly, the evening of frivolity takes on a bitter cast. All the gimmicks in the world can't compensate for the fact that love, or even the potential for a date, just doesn't materialize.

Each new gimmick that seems to put us on new ground and make it easier to meet people has the effect of driving home the basic reality of dating: it is difficult to meet people at all, let alone people whom we might actually love. Doing so under extreme circumstances might seem to be a solution to the problem, which is that we haven't managed to meet a great love under regular circumstances. But there would seem to be some fuzzy logic there.

HurryDate, like the other speed-dating hosts out there, boasts successful relationships that have sprung from its introductions. The same is true of people who set up their friends on blind dates. There are always success stories, and that is what we focus on. It's what keeps us coming back for more, even though the last time didn't quite work out.

There is no special magic to speed-dating. It is the basic law of probability: if you throw enough people in a room together, some of them are bound to like one another. And to help bear that out, several times a week for the next twelve months, HurryDate sends me e-mails inviting me to more events.

part three

dating in a high-tech world

For the past ten years, Barrett has led the life of a workaholic bachelor. He's watched friend after friend morph from college drinking buddy to married guy with new priorities on Saturday nights. He's worked hard, rising in just a few years to vice president at a consulting firm, and he has been on dozens, if not hundreds, of dates. "Part of the problem is I am just exhausted at the thought of regular dating," says Barrett, thirty-five, bemoaning the string of blind dates set up by well-meaning married friends.

Barrett meets Heidi online and trades e-mails with her for a couple of months. "I could tell from the nature of her responses that she was clearly crazy," Barrett says. "She'd give very short responses to my questions or ask me questions. But then she'd give no information in return. But she was by far the best-looking woman I'd seen on the site."

Barrett and Heidi decide to meet. "At some point, she asked if I liked shopping and told me she really needed some shoes." Barrett tells Heidi that maybe they can go shopping for some shoes when they get together. "I started to have a different attitude about it. I just started to think it would be one of those strange first dates. I figured I'd take her out and if I have to buy her some shoes, I'll buy her some shoes. And I'll have sex with her in the shoes and that will be it."

A week later, Barrett and Heidi go out for coffee and end up at a large department store having a sale. Heidi goes to look for some shoes. "She starts getting upset that she has little feet and she can't find any shoes that fit," Barrett recalls. But she says there's a lingerie sale upstairs. "If I find something I like, will you buy it for me?" she asks. Barrett agrees and proceeds to watch Heidi try on a wild assortment of lingerie. See-through teddies, bustier tops, lounge pants with no top. They make out in the dressing room.

They go out for Italian food, and Barrett tries to talk to Heidi. "It's just exhausting and brutal," Barrett says. "She was moody and upset but didn't articulate why. So I drove her home." Heidi proceeds to call Barrett's home and cell phone over and over for days. They talk a few times, and Barrett asks her out again. But the more he thinks about the concept of painful conversation, the more he knows he can't bear another date with Heidi. He calls her to cancel. "She just went ballistic. She starts swearing at me and saying, 'How dare you cancel on me for a Saturday night?'" Barrett puts up with a week during which time Heidi calls him fifteen times and shows up at his house unannounced before finally telling her, "This is unacceptable." He hasn't spoken to her since.

It has been a couple of months, and Barrett hasn't been checking the online profiles with any kind of consistency. "Fundamentally I don't have much faith or confidence in online dating. For all its potential, the realities of it make it no more effective than getting set up or meeting people other places," he says. "What's frustrating is here's this pool of women who describe what they're looking for in terms of looks and career, and I should be in the heart of the target zone for these women," says Barrett. "But there's no way to differentiate yourself. All the profiles start to sound the same, so even though there's this pool of people, it doesn't really help that much.

"The pace of relationships now is so fast with people trying to decide right off the bat whether it can work or not," Barrett goes on to say. "Sometimes I try to feel relaxed about it, to take the pressure feeling away. But if you seem too relaxed about it, it comes off as not being interested. I've tried the mellow, relaxed attitude and it doesn't work. I've tried it all."

. . . [A]ll lovers must realize that after the salutation they should not immediately begin talking about love, for it is only with their concubines that men begin in that way. On the contrary, after the man has greeted the woman he ought to let a little time elapse, so that she may, if she wishes, speak first.

FROM *The Art of Courtly Love*, BY ANDREAS CAPPELANUS, LATE 12TH CENTURY, TRANSLATION BY JOHN JAY PARRY

5.

ParisGal seeks travel partner who likes scrabble

"I am a loser," says Dan, as he looks at the J-Date homepage. "Seriously, I must have hit a new low. All I can think is that if I put up an ad, the *whole world* will know I am desperate," Dan says. He's contemplating the J-Date site because he's Jewish. In all the years he's dated and had girlfriends, none has ever shared the same religion with him. "The Jewish thing was never really a problem, but as long as I have the power to choose, why not be picky? Isn't that the whole point? I figured I might as well select the criteria I could never find in person." It's also a sign that Dan is more serious about potential dates. He's tired of relationships that lead nowhere and is hoping to meet "the last woman I'll ever date."

Before putting up his own profile, Dan, a thirty-three-year-old lawyer living in Los Angeles, scans the lists of smiling women whose profiles he can view for free. "The thing that amazes me was how many choices I suddenly have. There's no way I would be able to meet this many Jewish women in Los Angeles. I mean how would I find them? There's no central place where they all go," he says. Such is part of the appeal of online services. They have the ability to round up massive numbers of people of all ages, religions, and personality types. "I never had this problem in college. Everyone was my age, and there were tons of opportunities to meet people," says Dan, adding facetiously, "but the pool of applicants has dried up."

It's true. Once we get out into the world, no such forum exists to gather single adults together. The bigger the city, the bigger the problem. In the largest urban areas, we are often living far from where we grew up. We are missing the social networks of friends and family who might introduce us to one another. We have responsibilities. We have jobs. We can't spend each day trying to find people to date, let alone people who share common interests. In short, we may be surrounded by single men and women, but we simply can't find them.

Dan hems and haws for months before posting a profile on J-Date. "Eventually, I have to swallow my fear. I'm not meeting anyone, sitting home every night, so as much as I want to vomit, I'm going to put this ad here to tell the world I'm single."

Dan's reaction surprises him. The moment he hits the POST button and sends his profile into cyberspace, he is immediately overcome with a feeling of relief. "I felt like I had joined the party," he says. "So if there's someone out there who is surfing the Internet, looking for a guy like me, maybe she'll find me now." Dan says that he's no longer bothered by the idea that anyone posting an online ad is some sort of loser. "I figure that anyone who is a member of an online dating service is already part of it, so they won't think I'm lame if I'm part of it, too."

Mimi, thirty-six, who works for a nonprofit organization in San Francisco, has considered online dating but has so far rejected it because it feels too artificial. But her friends, single and married alike, are pushing her to open her mind to the concept. "Tonight was yet another night when someone close to me practically strapped me down and gave me the talk," Mimi says. "They say, 'This is so silly. You're so great about going out on blind dates, so why don't you try the Internet?'" It feels contrived, she says. But above all else, Internet dating lacks privacy. There is the persistent feeling that a friend or coworker could stumble upon Mimi's profile online and know she has sunk to what she perceives as the lowest of the low in her search for dates. "The main reason is that it feels like a job interview rather than a social life," she says.

another vivacious brunette

I can understand exactly how Mimi feels. The thought of registering myself for online dating feels like work. I wonder what it will take to bring me the same comfort level as Dan. Right now, I am paralyzed. I have been staring at my computer screen for an inordinately long time. This is a new sort of writer's block—the clammed-up, nervous feeling I have now. I can't decide whether to take the plunge.

My discomfort strikes on many levels. There is the slight feeling of embarrassment at placing an ad—however hip and trendy the medium—to tell the online world and anyone who browses there that I need help finding dates. There is the fear, no matter how remote, that someone I know will be browsing the dating site, see my picture, and conclude that my dating life has come to this. Placing an ad seems to tell the world I have failed to meet anyone "the normal way."

And there are other layers of anxiety. The sheer public nature of Internet dating strikes on a different plane. It feels risky to put personal information on the Web for potentially anyone to find. Is there a chance some weirdo will be able to track me down, based solely on my picture and the information I provide?

And there is the discomfort of a lie. I am not single and searching for love. And any man who responds to my ad will not be given directions to a secret rendezvous spot. Moreover, I am not a single, thirty-two-year-old woman in New York City searching for a man between the ages of 30 and 38. But the Internet frees me up to say one thing and to be entirely another, which highlights one of the biggest risks of opening ourselves up to dating in an anonymous venue like cyberspace. We have no idea who we're dealing with.

Those people who claim to own the moon and who have a profile and photo to prove it might not be who they say they are, either. They could be predators looking for lonely single men and women. They could be married and surfing the online personals for sport. They could be old and claiming to be young. They could be men claiming to be women. They could be you. They could be me. But we have to take them at face value on the Internet. Our gut instinct is all we have.

It would be very easy to overthink this. There are many people who would never dream of posting an online ad and certainly wouldn't imagine themselves responding to one. There are almost as many who used to feel this way and who are now dating someone they met on the Web.

Online dating sites have exploded in the past two years, with $449 million spent in 2003, a 49 percent increase over the prior year, according to comScore Networks, a Web tracking firm. The growth in activity, led by the most popular services—Match.com (a unit of IAC/InterActiveCorp), Yahoo! Personals, and Match Net Inc. sites (which include J-Date and Americansingles.com)—makes online personals one of the fastest-growing online businesses, estimated to reach $642 million in 2008, according to Jupiter Research. About eight million online daters are visiting the Web sites while at work, spending 51 minutes surfing for dates, compared to 37 minutes spent by those surfing Web personals from home, says comScore.

And if I am going to join them, I need to get over my initial anxiety.

hitting SEND

I choose Match.com because it is the biggest online dating site, with nearly one million paying members, and because it doesn't segment the dating population by religion or cultural preference. Still in stealth mode, I camp out on Match.com's homepage for several minutes, looking at pictures of women who have posted profiles. They're cheery and outgoing, smiling and inviting. They make it seem like there's nothing to it. I read one of their profiles: "Some people find me serious or even a little reserved, but I can be very silly. I have a good sense of humor and I love to laugh. I like going out, listening to music, just having fun. . . . My ideal match is someone who is fun and knows how to laugh at life, which, admit it, can be a little crazy sometimes."

Another writes, "I love activities such as hiking, biking, Rollerblading, and snowboarding. I also like staying in bed on rainy days and watching movies all day and cuddling with that special someone." There's something mildly comforting about being able to see who's been there first, posting a profile, bravely paving the way for others to do the same. It's almost as though we're part of a club. Only we online daters have to know about it.

"The appeal of dating online, from a marketing point of view, is that you don't have to advertise to the general public. You have the right target audience," says Jack, a thiry-five-year-old management consultant whose perspective on dating bespeaks his business school education. "The Internet is all about lead generation," he says. "I could go to a party or to a bar where there's no telling how old or how educated the women I meet will be, but online I can choose."

To Pamela, originally from Argentina, searching with specific criteria in mind is a distinctly American phenomenon. In Latin America, she says, men and women go out in groups and get to know one another. "There may be someone you like who you see in a group with other friends," Pamela says. "You are not really dating but you can decide if you want to spend time alone.

"American guys are very serious. If they meet you, they want to date you. They are not interested in being just friends. If I say

I am not interested in dating, they are gone. Latin guys would not be like that," adds Pamela, thirty-seven. "In Argentina, nobody counts dates like here. Nobody says, 'We're on our fourth date.' It's not so official. It's very American to have everything so measured." She concludes: "It is very American, the need to quantify the time we spend together as a certain kind of relationship. There is a need for results here."

Jack is the first to admit he is focused on results. For him, and many others searching online, there is a comfort level that comes with knowing everyone on a dating Web site is eligible and hoping to meet someone. "I think American men are afraid of rejection," says Jack, thirty-five, who lives in Los Angeles. "But this way, I can stack the deck in my favor." He can read the descriptions of what attributes a woman is looking for in a future boyfriend and size up whether he fits the bill. "Otherwise, I could spend a half hour talking to a woman at a party and hearing about her fascinating job at a marine sanctuary and her clever take on current events, only to learn fifteen minutes into a conversation that she has a boyfriend."

armchair dating

There is something enticing about introducing myself to the online world from the privacy of home. It's just me, sitting alone in front of the computer, trying to put my best foot forward for a host of strangers. Online dating, both in the early introduction stages and in the later weeks as relationships develop via e-mail, has brought dating back into the private realm.

Generations before us pushed to do away with dating that was confined to the sitting room or the front porch, and we are again bringing it back to the home front. Posting a profile and photo on the Internet for potential millions of onlookers to see is a very public act on one hand, but on the other, the nature of e-mailed correspondence gives us back the concept of privacy. We control whom we meet and whether we pursue relationships at all. Without ever meeting in person.

I type in a zip code for a neighborhood near my own and look at the selection of men that the site pulls up almost instantly. Match.com allows any visitor to do a limited search by age range and zip code without ever having to pay a dime, disclose any personal information, or register with the service. It is the first step toward reeling in the timid.

I have the same question everyone has when first considering any kind of service related to dating: who are the people who are doing this? There's a mixed sensation of fear that enlisting the help of a dating service firmly places us among the ranks of the biggest losers in history and the feeling of excitement that we are part of a truly cutting-edge dating scene. Using a dating service might be the only thing standing between us and true love.

Online dating is not humiliating because it's completely anonymous. There's no need for your friends, parents, or neighbors to know what you're up to until you hit pay dirt. And once you do, you become the stuff of legend. Almost everyone knows people who met the man or woman of their dreams through an online dating site. It's hard to refute a success story.

But there are success stories for almost anything: women have succeeded at wooing a bachelor on network television; men have succeeded at ordering Russian brides. There are blind dates that end in marriage, and matchmakers who swear by their trade. Just because there have been romances sprung from the trenches of online dating services, does it mean it is the new way single people are meant to meet each other? And is there some reason why it shouldn't be?

All the stories and secondhand information are purely anecdotal. From what I can tell, online dating has to be experienced to be understood. I pick a screen name.

wading into the deep end

Now I am ParisGal. I hope there is nothing in my choice of screen name that will unintentionally reveal too much or too little about me. I like Paris. I figure I will at least have something in common with someone who responds to my profile simply because he, too, likes Paris. But there is nothing deep-seated in my distinction between calling myself a woman, a womyn, a girl, a gal, or a sea turtle. I could just as easily have been TurtleGal. Maybe I should have been. But for all intents and purposes here my screen name is mildly representative of me without being too much of anything.

The adjectives I choose are more or less descriptive of myself. I change a few biographical details for the sake of maintaining my anonymity, most significantly my zip code. I choose a New York zip code so I will not run the risk of my next-door neighbor finding me in a search of women my age in a 50-mile radius.

Part of the appeal of crafting an online version of ourselves is that we have the freedom to embellish on our best qualities and downplay the ones we could live without. Who wouldn't relish the chance to put his or her best foot forward? It's like sending a résumé to a potential employer. We are trying to get noticed, trying to distinguish ourselves from the pile.

There is only so much I can do to distinguish myself, however, because I am given a choice of adjectives to describe myself and boxes to check to describe my build, hair color, religious preference, and other biographical tidbits. I can characterize my sense of humor as anything from gentle to sarcastic, my taste in clothes as trendy to classic. I am relieved that I am simply being asked to check boxes, rather than come up with a way to describe my idea of fun or the state of cleanliness in my house.

But then comes the obligatory paragraph where I need to describe my winning attributes in no fewer than two hundred characters and no more than one thousand. I am supposed to come up with enough unusual but not downright scary tidbits that will intrigue someone enough to answer my ad. Easier said than done.

It is hard to write something that doesn't sound either wistfully sappy and/or purely biographical. For some reason, all that comes to mind are Pollyanna-inspired quips along the lines of "romantic gal seeks soul mate who loves sunsets and walks on the beach." After all, who doesn't love sunsets? I soon discover that many of the members of this particular dating service are in the market for a fellow sunset watcher or beach walker. It is a universal pursuit.

As I look for inspiration from profiles posted by other women, it strikes me that a lot of us describe ourselves the same way. "I guess I would describe myself as easygoing and funny. I have a lighthearted personality and I love to laugh!" says one.

I look at another: "I'm attractive with medium-length brown hair, nice eyes, and a great smile. I'm serious but I also love to laugh, especially at myself. I can pretty much find humor in most situations. I also love to cook, especially when it's cooking dinner for that special someone."

And another: "I'm a pretty, petite, athletic female who is intelligent and compassionate. I like to laugh (even at myself) but know when to be serious."

It turns out a lot of women are fond of laughter.

I look at one more: "I am passionate about many things but one of my favorites is cooking. Just ask my friends, who are frequent guests! I'm an easygoing woman who loves to have fun. I'm looking to share some good times and laughter with a nice man." It is unanimous.

In creating his profile, Jack tries to list tangibles that people could respond to. He mentions that he worked in the Peace Corps. He describes himself as an investment banker and someone who meditates and does yoga every day—"things that someone would respond to if she were looking for someone like me," he says.

"I really approached it like a business proposition," Jack goes on to say. He reads women's profiles to see what they're looking for and reads other men's profiles to see the kinds of things they write. "I even called the company to ask if there were certain things people wrote that seemed to work better than others. If I'm going to invest the time in dating online, I want to be successful," he says. "Most people don't describe themselves with distinct traits, so a lot of them end up sounding the same. I eliminate those right off the bat."

who am i?

As I struggle to come up with something, I become the embodiment of every stereotypical personal ad I've ever seen. I want to call myself adventurous. I consider saying I am easygoing. I even come frighteningly close to calling myself a passionate lover of something or other. A passionate lover of dogs. Of frogs. Of clogs.

I think about writing about nothing in particular, like describing in detail the process of going from room to room, sweeping the dog hair from the house. Or discussing the way I make pasta with kalamata olives and goat cheese. Anything—just to fill the space. But I know that my efforts to appear mysterious, odd, or overly clever will be exactly that. And what's more, there will be a certain roster of guys who will find this appealing, simply because it is different.

Meeting online essentially provides all participants with the chance to put forward the best possible impressions: the nicest photo they can scrounge up, the best summary paragraph that communicates who they are and how they want to be perceived, the most accurate adjectives from the selection provided by the Web site itself.

Some people take full advantage and post a really nice photo. Others clearly are snapping a digital photo of themselves on the fly, evidenced by the appearance of their faces looking slightly upward and the length of an arm barely visible on the edge of the photo. Some write a detailed description of themselves and their outlook on the world, as well as the qualities they're looking for in a life partner. Others write a quick biographical note, clearly not wanting to venture much, as if not much will ultimately be gained.

Match.com allocates forty-five minutes for anyone to post a profile. After that time, they automatically log out any user who isn't finished, for security purposes. I can't imagine that I will need forty-five minutes. After deleting several versions, I settle on a paragraph I can live with. It takes me fifteen minutes.

My personal statement: "I'm an outgoing, introspective lover of Paris, San Francisco, and many tiny towns in between. I'm equally comfortable living life at a breakneck pace or slowing down to watch the tides roll in and out. I put no stock in fortune cookies, but I believe the Magic 8 Ball knows all. I'm looking for a guy who likes long dinner conversations, the occasional heated debate, and a good late-night game of Scrabble. Brains and a sense of humor are key. I'm a huge fan of traveling, hiking until my legs are Jell-O, running on the beach with big dogs, and sleeping late. My idea of fun is hiking to the bottom of the Grand Canyon and back in a day, then making quesadillas over an open fire and taking a two-hour nap—can you keep up? I'm petite but strong, occasionally funny, always open to new ideas."

And for the description of my ideal mate: "I'm looking for a guy who knows how to have a good time, who's willing to travel the world on a shoestring budget, and who has the desire to take breaks from work, at least occasionally. Sense of humor is essential—the rest is negotiable."

Is my profile an honest portrayal of myself? Actually, yes. At least, it's the self I am when not stressed out by where my career is headed at any given moment or by friends who have annoyed me by betraying confidences. It is the way I'd describe myself on a good day, when only my positive qualities are evident and any negative ones are neatly disguised. How many of us can do that when we meet someone in person? It is the self I truly am. It's just that I cannot always be that self. None of us can. Given the chance, was I going to tell anyone haunting the profiles on Match.com that I could do with some sit-ups and I've never understood what happened with Enron? Of course not.

When asked to write a one-paragraph description of ourselves, most of us would include the qualities we wish we had more of, even if they are only a few of the qualities we actually possess. A more honest description of myself would admit that I am almost always worried about something. I love to travel, but I often get so bogged down with work that I don't take that trip I've been meaning to go on for years. I'm lighthearted but I occasionally get moody and I don't even know why. A sense of humor is important, but dumb punch lines annoy me. How many of us would characterize ourselves as lovers of big dogs and running on the beach, yet live dog-free, landlocked lives?

The image we project is only one-half of the truth. But it is our best half. Maybe if we start off by exchanging descriptions of our ideal selves, we are that much closer to becoming them.

here we lie

Those half-truths do not go unnoticed. "Pretty much every woman who puts her profile online checks the box describing herself as lean and slender. And of all the women I've met through dating sites, not one is actually lean and slender," says Dan. "'Athletic and fit' could mean a porker with a tip-top cardiovascular system."

There is a certain element of fantasy when it comes to creating online profiles for ourselves. Since Web surfers are actually none the wiser until they meet us in person, there's ample temptation to make ourselves sound better and even look better than we actually do in person. "The picture is always either ten years old, or it's by far the best picture they've ever taken in their lives," says Dan.

"When the whole system is based on pseudonyms and aliases, people do not depict themselves accurately," says Jonathan Abrams, founder of Friendster.com, an online dating and networking service which only allows friends of friends to contact one another after being included in their circles of online friends. "If you're there in front of your friends, there's more accountability; you're likely to be more accurate." The system of friends vouching for friends has its appeal, evidenced by Friendster's growth to more than one million users in its first year.

But in some ways, lying is encouraged. The whole point of posting profiles of ourselves is to create an enticing advertisement. If a woman downplays her attributes in the hope of seeming humble, it's quite possible that no one will give her the time of day. Especially when the profiles before and after her make the other members sound like the next coming of Aphrodite. But the result can be disappointment. "One woman told me that I'm the first guy she's gone out with who actually looked like his picture," says Dan. "That immediately made me think I should put up a better picture because people must be assuming that I look much worse and that somehow I was able to scrounge up this halfway decent picture. And then I wanted to kick myself for thinking that way. I should be able to put up a picture that looks like me and have that be the right thing to do."

Beyond the lies about our looks, there is additional online fibbing going on. For some that comes in the form of subtracting a couple years from our true age, adding a few thousand to our annual incomes, or even saying we are single when we are in relationships.

"I met someone who told me she'd marked the profile box saying she has or would like to have a dog, and this guy wrote her a whole e-mail from the perspective of his dog, telling her why she should date the dog's owner," says Dan. "She thought it was kind of cute and original so they went on a date. And it turned out the guy would just send out the same e-mail to anyone he was interested in, inserting whichever pet she put in her profile. So if she had a bird, he'd be writing from the perspective of his bird. He didn't even have a dog," Dan says. "These are the kinds of people I'm up against."

In some cases, the lies are more subtle. It can be a question of intentions: some people post profiles in hope of developing an online relationship, having no intention of actually meeting in person. And to someone who is hoping for an in-person relationship, it can be a source of false hope when a steamy e-mail exchange begins. Michelle, a gay woman in her early forties, has been corresponding with a woman she met on a dating Web site two months ago. "But she refuses to make a date to get together," says Michelle, who really likes her potential partner but who is tired of meeting people who are so guarded. "This reminds me of another relationship I had two years ago. It took me six months to get her to a comfort level where she wanted to meet in person. And then we dated for a year." Michelle is hoping her new e-mail correspondence will turn out like the other one, but she's starting to have doubts. "I think she may just want an e-mail buddy and she's afraid to tell me," she says. "It's too bad, though, because I really like her."

art thou romeo?

Once I get through lying about myself, it is time to describe what I am looking for in a potential match. I am close to throwing in the towel. Who cares? Send me anyone you've got—I'll sift through them later. I check as few boxes as possible, leaving the choice of political affiliation, religion, race, and physical characteristics up to chance.

Next I pick a pricing plan. People have different strategies for using the services of a dating site. The conservative approach is to sign up for one month at $24.95. Then if all goes well and romance blooms or if all goes horribly and we need to abort mission, there is only a month's investment at stake. But there is an advantage to signing up for several months at once, because the per-month charge drops to $19 with a three-month membership, even less with a six-month membership, and so on. Signing up for the full-year plan brings the price down to $13 a month.

But by signing up for a year's worth of dating, are we saying that we can't imagine meeting someone inside of a year? None of us wants to think that we could still be searching in a year. That's like making a New Year's Eve buddy date on January 15 for the following year. Anyone who's single and hoping to meet someone enters a new year with the hope and, more important, the conviction that this will be the year for it. Signing up for the buddy date a year in advance just seems defeatist. So does signing up for a year's worth of online dating, dollar-savvy or not.

This is how online dating services make their money. They bank on our hope that one month will be enough. And if that doesn't work, we sign up for one more month. And possibly one more. By then we've spent $75, and we're halfway toward our full-year fee, but somehow it feels better. More hopeful. I choose the one-month plan.

For my initial online dating foray, I will post a profile without a photo. Match.com doesn't exactly discourage this, but it does observe that users who post a picture receive eight times more responses than those who don't. I can understand why. Most of us, when given the choice between someone we can see in photo form and someone we can't would choose the less camera-shy of the two. There's the unfortunate assumption that anyone who decides not to post a photo does so for fear of frightening away any decent prospects with a face only a monkey's mother could love. Or that he or she is inept at uploading a simple graphics file. But I am not ready to have my grinning mug posted for any member of the general public who happens to type in a zip code in some proximity to mine. It's all too easy.

And it's not for everyone. "I just tried Lavalife," says Mary, forty-one, who works in the entertainment industry in Los Angeles, "and I found it horrifying—the idea that you don't know who anyone is. You're just looking at their pictures and what they say about themselves." Mary hasn't been able to bring herself to e-mail any of the men whose profiles she finds on Lavalife, and she hasn't responded to the ones who've contacted her. She only signed up because her friends and family were bugging her to do something about her single status. "But, literally, the idea of having to send in a picture is so horrifying that I couldn't do it," she says. Mary got her Visa bill and saw the $28 charge for the service and was annoyed she had paid for it. "It's so disconnected from the experience of meeting people, the idea of writing to someone in response to an ad. To me each one is a potential failure as opposed to a potential experience," she says.

That's true of dating in general. "I won't go take a class because I might meet people," says Mimi in San Francisco. "I will take a class because I want to take a class. I just joined a gym in the heart of the Castro in San Francisco. There are probably five or six straight people who belong to this gym, and I find that very appealing," Mimi says. "I can do what I'm there to do. But I have been so roundly chastised by friends and my mother for joining a gym that is all gay and lesbian. But truth be told, I wasn't ever going to meet anyone at the gym."

Mimi faces the paradox shared by many men and women who have careers they've worked hard at and social lives that are the pity of their married friends. "I'm successful and independent and head of an organization, but I'm everyone's charity case," Mimi says. "I hate that I've become that, but that's the only way I meet people, so I depend on it. But I don't like being that person." She is the "single friend" who stands on the receiving end of a relentless slew of single prospects provided by friends, family, and colleagues. "Anyone who doesn't have a tail has been given my phone number."

Mary says she'd rather be fixed up "the old fashioned way. I'd rather talk on the phone, set a time to meet. I had a recent fix-up, and the guy said he'd e-mail me a picture. He sent a picture of himself in a Chippendales outfit. I guess he was thinking that was cute, but I found it so off-putting," Mary says.

It's a common feeling. For now, I'm satisfied entering the dating world in relative obscurity, photo-free. Besides, I am curious to see whether anyone will respond to me if I only write a one-paragraph introduction and check the boxes that are provided to me. Do we live in a virtual world where actual looks are important? Even when we are not face-to-face, do faces matter?

I post my ad and wait.

venus, if you will

The next day, Match.com sends me a welcoming e-mail from "Venus" and a list of prospective dates, ten altogether. Every few days, I'm told, Venus will send me another list of ten men who match the criteria I set forth. Then I have the option of e-mailing them or waiting to see if anyone will e-mail me. Women have the luxury of laziness when it comes to making contact. As is often true in the nonvirtual world, it is frequently a man who does the initial asking and only the bolder few women who take the reins.

I look at each profile of the men sent my way. I have matches from every corner of the nation, men of varying ages, religions, educational backgrounds. My potential matches live everywhere from Tulsa to Jersey City. This is partially a function of the broad criteria I selected when describing an ideal match. Surely, if I were really seeking to make a match, I'd have some criteria other than insisting they be male.

The first candidate, who goes by the name EZCharlie200, says, "Like most city dwellers, I play a game of chicken with the gym and take comfort in the physical benefits working out brings." He has brown hair and lives in Oklahoma. He works in the health sciences field. He says he is spiritual but not religious, and categorizes his living space as "always clean for company."

The next "match," a man with the screen name Slackjaw, says, "Most likely you will never meet another guy on this planet who is exactly like me because of my nonjudgmental nature. I bring balance and freedom to a relationship and value truth, lightness, and clarity above all else." He goes on to describe his value system, which, not surprisingly, includes balance. Plus, he adds, "I don't take myself too seriously." He has blond hair, likes dogs and cats, and doesn't like reptiles or fleas. He is a Latter-day Saint and describes his fashion sense as "designer—labels are a sign of fashion and style that are worth paying for." And at parties, he says, he is a social butterfly.

I realize I am not the only one who had a hard time coming up with a vaguely human-sounding self-description. There are a lot of attempts to come across as a sincere, easygoing guy who loves adventure.

Other examples of computer-generated matches for my criteria include a man who compares himself to a low-mileage truck, another who believes in "creating movement to keep life from being stagnant," a third who loves to let Mother Nature shine upon him. It is very difficult to write a profile that doesn't sound goofy, overly earnest, or simply odd or that doesn't read like a résumé of activities.

Online dating is different than meeting someone through a friend, where there's some degree of recourse and someone to vouch for a person's good upbringing. Even meeting a stranger in a bar provides some level of information. "You can learn something from their posture, who they are with, why they're there," Jack says. "If they're there for a friend's birthday, they might not be party people, but if they go to bars as their activity, it says something else about them."

Jack has adjusted his concept of relationships, necessitated by the online environment. Relationships take longer to develop when two people meet anonymously. "When you meet in person, you are dealing with the data firsthand," Jack says. There is no way to know just by exchanging e-mails what a person is really like—even if he or she has an unusual screen name and a witty conversational style. Eventually, it comes down to a gut feeling. "You have to hear their voice in a profile," Jack says. "You need to establish ties to something other than a common interest in dating. It's a bit much to have that as the main strong mutual interest. The stakes become really high."

To be sure, dating Web sites can double as online pickup joints, where some people are looking only for sex. But many other participants say they want to find a soul mate, a special person to settle down with. The profiles make it clear that their authors mean business. They are tired of just dating. Dating the wrong people or dating as a way to pass an evening has worn thin. They are delineating their qualifications very carefully and asking only well-equipped candidates to apply.

But everyone, it seems, is whimsical and loves adventure. "I am a very adventurous person, both in my work and personal life. All that is missing is someone to share the sunsets with," writes one. "I totally believe in love at first sight as any true romantic would," says another. And a third: "I can attend a black tie event or rough it at a desolate wilderness location."

Ninety percent of the men whose profiles I read have checked the box which describes their sense of humor as "witty—nothing's better than razor-sharp verbal repartee." Not that they actually employ their razor-sharp wit in the paragraphs they later use to describe themselves. Wit must not be squandered. As hard as it is to convey in one paragraph the complex beings that we each are, a surprising amount of personality comes through. Even a few sentences of description reveal whether the writer is trying to sound smart, overly cultured, intimately sincere, or even intimidated.

Lookin4Yew says his ideal match "would be someone who embraces life for all its beauty and flaws, someone who greets each morning with uncompromising fervor." He always puts in overtime at work and when meeting a friend, he is fashionably late. His sense of humor is, by his own admission, "witty."

selling ourselves

In looking through the matches that were selected for me, it becomes clear that there are common themes in what we want to project to the opposite sex. Many men describe themselves as gourmet cooks or simply as loving to make dinner for someone special. They emphasize romance and their desire to focus on a good conversation, on a relationship. For their part, women often emphasize their desire to have a good time. Dating Web sites are a mecca for men and women with wanderlust and All-Clad cookware. It seems like every other profile I look at hits on either travel, cooking, or curling up somewhere or other as a favorite pastime. I can't help but wonder whether these are the most apt descriptions or just what we think potential dates want to hear.

When the men describe what they are looking for in a woman, some present simple portraits of a pleasant, attractive person, while others seem to have constructed a Svengali princess in their minds. Browneyes21 says he's looking for a woman who doesn't use the word "party" as a verb. He wants to sit by a fire and talk all night long. He's open to women who speak languages ranging from English and French to Urdu and Tagalog. And he doesn't mind pets.

It is hard to strike a balance between saying something original and sounding just plain weird. Most men land somewhere between the two. GottaLuvNY describes himself in capital letters: "REAL. I have laughed, I have cried. I know my joy, I know my tears. I want to love without boundaries and feel the beauty in the darkness of pain. I view my sorrows as a voyage I am lucky to travel alone or with a (hopefully) partner." When we are given freedom to describe ourselves, some of us get carried away.

Dating online requires each of us to have a sales pitch. We're supposed to distinguish ourselves from the pack, and we want to show there's more to us than a photo and biographical stats. The same guy who prattles on about his depth of character and his love for aching and bitterness counters a few sentences later by. saying, "I can find levity and humor in anything and love to have a good time." It's hard to fit our multifaceted selves into one thousand words or less.

For his part, Jack narrows down the profiles to those he wants to approach. Looks are a factor, he notes, as are education and interests. "You learn a lot when you go to write something to someone," Jack says. "If you have nothing to say after reading her profile, that says something.

"Many women say, 'I can do a night on the town and also sit on the couch in my sweats.' That doesn't tell me anything," Jack says. "I want to know what you're watching when you're sitting on the couch. Are you watching *Buffy the Vampire Slayer* and do you think I'm going to watch with you? And when you go out, are you dancing on the tables or are you sitting back and observing the crowd?" he says.

And then he gets honest. "At the end of the day, you look at the picture and make a decision."

Love-letters are ever a mixture of bitter and sweet, and frequently fail to satisfy either party.

But a profusion of curious conceits and quotations are not suited to their character, as true sentiment is usually direct and to the point; and does not stray into the by-ways of literature to gather the flowers of rhetoric.

FROM *A Manual of Etiquette with Hints on Politeness and Good Breeding,* BY DAISY EYEBRIGHT (A PSEUDONYM FOR SOPHIA ORNE JOHNSON), 1873

6.

i've got mail

A couple days after I post my profile, a few intrepid souls make contact.

I open the first e-mail and gain an immediate understanding why it's so hard to meet someone this way. Gordon, the first guy to respond, tells me, "I LOVED your profile. You definitely sound like someone I would love to know more about." He goes on to tell me he is a certified masseur and a gourmet cook. He signs his note, "Yours," with hugs and kisses by way of x's and o's.

The second note, from Bill, says he was intrigued by my profile. "I just had to discover who this person was, to discover the special person that she might be. I hope you understand that and can hear who I am coming through to you as you read this e-mail.

It's so difficult to find intelligent people. Too often I meet people who talk endlessly about nothing; you look deep into their eyes and you get the feeling there is nothing there. No intelligence or personality. But, you know how, every now and then, you meet someone, and you can tell right away, from the way they talk, act, or write, that they actually *think* [sic] about life and the things that matter; that this is someone who you could find yourself talking to late into the night and sharing with each other the things you've each learned about life."

All this earnestness, and Bill gets nothing from me. I'm soliciting responses to my ad when I have no intention of going out with anyone. Bill goes on, "So, listen, if any of this has caught your attention and as you begin to think more and more about what you need, you find yourself excited to have the opportunity to get to know me better, please feel free to take all the time you need to respond right now and tell me how you feel." How do I feel? I feel rotten. I feel guilty.

In reality, many of the people who are using online dating sites are already in relationships, whether "they're on a break" or they're testing the waters in anticipation of a future breakup. But the feeling persists that there should be honesty here. Even if the online dating arena isn't one that requires it.

I open up e-mail number three. "Hello Worldly Traveler. . . . don't you love it?!! I've done a lot of the things that you mentioned, like the Grand Canyon, so we might click. . . ." Sid's e-mail talks about travel plans and conveys his hang-loose persona. It concludes, "Ciao for now babe. . . ."

Three different men, three entirely different responses. It becomes immediately clear how hard it would be to meet someone this way. How much can you tell from an e-mailed missive? Even when there is a complete profile, with photo, to back it up? It's also hard to tell what people use as a basis for their decision to respond. According to a survey of more than eight thousand of its members, Match.com says 31 percent of respondents listed age as the most important aspect of a profile, while 34 percent admitted to judging body type as most crucial. The remaining responses were divided among ethnicity, education, and income.

I wait three more days to see if anyone else will contact me, based purely on my photo-free presence on the Match.com site. I realize this is a passive approach. I could surf the Match site myself and look for like-minded souls. But I am lazy. "Women tend to sit back and wait for men to respond," says Priscilla Chang, former director of marketing for Match.com. "The ones you're going to want to talk to are the ones who aren't that aggressive, the ones who don't use the shotgun approach." But I stick to my passive ways. Days go by. Nothing.

For men, the statistics are even worse. One man I interview tells me he posted a photo-less ad and left it up for three months. He received no responses. The statistics are not much better for men who do post photos; for all the cutting-edge mentality encouraged by online dating, we still fall back on heavy tradition where the man does the asking.

Of course, there is the more dire possibility: maybe it's just harder these days for men. In a twist on the 1986 *Newsweek* article that said a college-educated woman had a better chance of being killed by a terrorist than getting married after forty, a 2001 *Wall Street Journal* article explored the possibility of a woman shortage which could leave more men single over the ensuing decades. The assertion is based on U.S. Census Bureau data predicting that by 2010, men in their late thirties and early forties will outnumber women five to ten years younger by two to one. With the odds possibly against them, men certainly don't have the luxury of posting a photo-less ad. They need to do all they can to distinguish themselves. Apparently so do I.

I face facts. Posting an ad without a photo is akin to going to a party with a bag over my head. While there are a few men who might be intrigued, most turn the other way. The Internet is a visual medium, and while some people might be willing to correspond without first seeing a picture, most want to bring the relationship quickly out of the virtual realm and into the real one. And putting a face to the description is the first way to make that happen.

inciting an avalanche

No one wants to look like he's trying too hard. Many of the men and women interviewed for this book say they don't want to spend too much time on their profiles. They don't want to waste a lot of time on something that may come to naught, and they don't want to appear to be spending more time than they should trying to solicit interest in themselves.

Pamela, the education consultant from Argentina, posts her profile on Match.com and is immediately overwhelmed by the number of men who respond to her profile. "What is the point of all these guys contacting me online because they like my profile?" she asks. "What am I going to do with two hundred guys?" Realistically, she's not going to go out on two hundred dates in a week, so she needs to sort through the responses. "Most are sending out e-mails to tons of women indiscriminately, so they're just playing the odds, playing with the laws of probability," Pamela says. She likens the process to looking for an apartment. "When I was driving around in neighborhoods, I'd see one or two apartments I liked and filled out applications. I'd see a couple other people doing the same. They were my competition," she says. Then she signed up with a rental-search company. She got a list of twenty-five apartments, all of which sounded great. But when she went to see them, she found dozens of people who'd all received the same rental list. More apartments, more competition. "I filled out applications at all of them and didn't get any of them," says Pamela. What's the point of abundance for abundance's sake?

When functioning as intended, online dating creates a problem of oversupply. It breeds a perception that there is a limitless trove of new dating possibilities, and it tempts us to dip continually into the pot for someone better. "I can't tell you how many times I've come home from a date I thought went well and looked at Match.com's Web site to find that the guy I just went out with is 'online now,' checking his e-mail or looking for new people to date," Pamela says. Internet dating feeds the perception that there is a constant stream of available dates for the picking.

There is something insidious about a dating service that engenders a continual sense that there's someone better out there, more attractive, more compatible, while offering a method for finding that person. What is the advantage of having a vast supply of potential dates at our disposal if we are never going to be satisfied with any one of them?

"I would rather get two dates or two apartments that have a chance of working out," Pamela says. "The Internet gives you the feeling of all these possibilities but it's more of an illusion."

I, on the other hand, am not finding quite the oversupply of men clamoring to meet me. Quite the contrary. I seem to have hit a roadblock. Day after day, I check my e-mail and find nothing except more of Match.com's picks. I guess the picture I painted of myself doesn't sound that intriguing after all. But it's all I've got. I had imagined that men would swoon over my Grand Canyon escapades and my quirky faith in the Magic 8 Ball. Instead they view my photoless profile merely as proof I'm ugly.

Of course, I could choose a niche online dating service like eHarmony, which markets itself as careful screeners of its members. The service makes members wait until they've established a level of compatibility with a potential date before revealing photos. Instead, I decide to post a photo. It's time to put myself on the line.

Still wanting to maintain some level of anonymity, I choose a picture of myself that is seven years old. Anyone who knows me would probably recognize me in the old photo, but it gives me some comfort knowing that a stranger on the street probably wouldn't be able to identify me from it, even if it were beaming down from a billboard over my head.

I wait for the photo to make its way past the screeners who check all material before it gets posted on the site to make sure none of us is trying to pass off a photo of Brad Pitt as our own. I plan to keep my profile with picture on the site for one week, after which time I will erase my online presence entirely and return to the dark ages of milling around the video store as a way of finding human contact.

an array of options

At dawn of a new day, I make the mistake of logging on to my computer before I've had a cup of coffee. I am not prepared for what comes next. I'm casually checking the news and opening my e-mail box when I get two instant messages from men who've seen that I'm online. I also get a message from Match.com telling me someone named Zen45 has "winked" at me. It's like a hornet's nest of B-12 bombers descending on an exposed target. I'm so inept at this that I have to go to the Match.com site and read the instructions. It turns out that I inadvertently checked a box that allows others to see when I'm online. And Zen45 is using a feature known on Match.com as a "wink," but also goes by the "smile," the "icebreaker," or the "hot list," depending on what service you use. I thought I was just going to get a few, plain old e-mails. Meanwhile Zen45 is sending me a winking icon to say he's interested without having to be so overt as to communicate with nouns and verbs. Or, heaven forbid, adjectives.

Turns out I am not the only one who's baffled by the inbreeding of technology. "What am I supposed to think when someone hot-lists me?" asks Dan. "I guess it means they liked my profile enough to click a button but not enough to take the time to write an e-mail. It's like a bartender coming over and saying the woman at the next table has bought me a drink." Dan acknowledges that it also may be less risky. We can hot-list each other without really putting ourselves on the line. "It's noncommittal; if a woman hot-lists me, she's leaving it up to me to look at her profile and make the opening move," Dan says.

And sometimes that move is a passive-aggressive one: hot-listing back. "I've had women hot-list me and I've decided I'd just put them on my hot list. Touché. Now it's her move," Dan says. Sometimes two hot-listers simply stare each other down without progressing further. "It's like dogs sniffing each other," Dan says. The added services can also have the effect of being too much information. Do I really want to log on to a dating Web site and be told that eight hundred people have viewed my profile when only three contacted me? "It can be depressing when you see how many people have 'viewed' you," says Dan. "I end up feeling bad about the ones who checked me out and moved on even though I've done the same thing myself."

As for myself, I am sufficiently overwhelmed that I log off and spend the rest of the day communicating using old-fashioned devices like parchment paper and wax seals. I turn my cell phone off and close the blinds. Maybe I'm not ready for high-tech dating.

another try

The music on my clock radio lulls me into the vague sense that I should open my eyes. Surprisingly, after a night filled with dreams about men on Match.com hiding in the bushes outside my window, I wake up refreshed. Intrepid. I have turned off the feature that allows Match.com members to instant-message me. So I am back in control. And I have a dozen new e-mails.

The new batch contains a broad array of messages. Some men write page upon page, telling me all the things they feel we have in common and suggesting that we get together soon. Others content themselves with saying hello and ask me to write back if I like their profiles. I look at them one by one. They are like job-interview candidates, each with a cover letter and résumé of interests and hobbies. The same rules apply: typos are a turnoff. And outright grammatical errors do not make a good first impression. Overzealousness gives an air of desperation. Lists of purely biographical information don't tell enough about a person.

E-mail number one reads, "Hello Pretty Lady!! Before I tell you about myself (and trust me, you won't be disappointed), I want to let you know that I read your profile very carefully and have to admit that I truly like your style!! You are obviously intelligent and attractive, but more than that I think that you are probably a lot of fun . . . in which case I would like to get to know you better. . . ." He goes on to tell me about his job as a stockbroker, his outlook on life (sunny), and his build, which he says is tall and muscular. He asks questions. He lists his private office line and his cell-phone number. He wants to know when we can get together, because he "can truly see how well we will hit it off." He talks about romance and all the options we have for contacting each other and getting together. He goes on for three pages. The stock market rises and falls again in the time he spends writing this note.

Some people come on strong and have a three-minute conversation all by themselves without waiting to see if the person they're talking to is interested. Others will send a subtle glance from across the room and abort mission if the glance isn't returned with enthusiasm. "Like the judges always say in court, right before I think I'm going to give a winning argument, 'Counselor, are you going to be telling me anything I can't read in your papers?'" says Dan, the lawyer. "Save your breath. Don't write a long e-mail. Just let them read your profile and go from there."

I open the second e-mail. It is a brief note from a man with the screen name BusyBobby, who says he's frequently in town on business and would love to have someone new to get to know. I can see how dating Web sites could be a breeding ground for future stalkers.

I move on to the third: "Hello. I really enjoyed your profile . . . and share your love of dogs. Sincerely, Donald."

And so on. E-mail number eight: "Hi, my name is John. I am an attorney. I read your profile and it sounded interesting. I snowboard in the winter and rock climb in the summers. I have attached my profile. If interested, e-mail me." John's e-mail is generic, much like a handful of the ones I would later receive. Many people say they have a stock e-mail they send to anyone whose profile catches their eye. They don't want to invest a lot of time in writing individualized missives to different people because the reality is that most will not get a reply. The individualized e-mails can come later, once both people have established at least a cursory interest.

Three days later, I get the same stock e-mail from John. Match.com's Venus feature sometimes sends the same profiles in more than one batch of ten matches. I can only imagine John forgot he has already contacted me.

E-mail number nineteen: "i love to travel . . . i been backpacking to europe on the smallest budget. we should talk. Kal."

I soon realize that "meeting" people through online personals is not really much different from meeting them in a bar or at a party, minus the awkward, stumbling introductions. Correction:

there are awkward stumbling introductions online as well. When it comes time to send an e-mail to someone appealing, things often fall apart. Here is where poor grammar and annoying e-mail habits like the excessive use of winking smiley faces can either entice or annoy. Same goes for an abundance of exclamation points which can make the sender seem either very excited or downright irate.

In the ancient world when relationships developed through telephone conversations and in-person meetings, there was no such thing as a misplaced modifier to indicate to a potential date that we're unsuitable. Grammatical mistakes are the spinach in the teeth of the Internet generation. They're a tiny piece of who we present ourselves to be, something that can be dissected and analyzed when there's a dearth of other information to go on. How patient and forgiving are we? Do we comment on the error? Relationships can live or die depending on the grammatical compatibility of the corresponding parties. Do we need to have compatible writing styles to be compatible in person?

"If a woman writes me an e-mail full of grammatical errors or even spelling mistakes, it bothers me. I can't help it," says Dan. He recalls an e-mail getting-to-know-you session that had been going well with a potential date, until she signed off one fateful time: "Toodles." "I don't know why but that just rubbed me the wrong way," Dan says. They never ended up going out on a date.

jack

Jack continues searching online. He finds someone he likes and starts e-mailing her. A few messages in, they move on to the phone. "I figure the phone call is going to tell you more in the first three minutes than a month of e-mails, so do what you can to get there," he says. "I'm not interesting in e-mailing indefinitely and if a woman seems like she has that proclivity, it's a bad sign." But Sandrine is happy to meet Jack for a drink. Jack notes that this is the first date he's been on where the woman in front of him actually looks better than the photo posted with her profile. She has straight blond hair, green eyes, and a smile that comes with some effort. "Within five minutes, our conversation turned into an interview," Jack says. "She wanted to know where I'm from, what my values are, whether I want to have kids, and whether I'm looking for a serious relationship." According to Match.com, 76 percent of men surveyed by the company say they're sized up as potential fathers on the first date.

Jack answers each question and watches Sandrine squint her eyes and tabulate the information with a mental checklist. "She didn't even listen to the ends of my answers to her questions. She'd cut me off three sentences into the paragraph." Could it be that we've gotten so used to the levels of screening and the ability to select for brown hair or right-wing conservatism that we've forgotten how to behave in person? Our business culture trains us to assess a situation quickly for its potential and determine whether it is a good investment of our time. But human relationships are nothing if not an investment of time.

"The problem with trying to meet someone who is 'ready for a relationship' is that a relationship can't develop at a natural pace," Jack says. "People who are ready to meet someone are overready." After about a half hour of questioning, Sandrine furrows her brow and tells Jack she's tired. "I asked her why she contacted me in the first place," Jack says, somewhat amused by the whole experience. "She said, 'You were kind of cute and didn't have a goatee.' That was the entire criteria."

pamela

Pamela meets Derrick at a party. They go out a few times but Pamela doesn't really consider them dates because she's not interested in him. But she likes him enough to spend time with him, so occasionally she'll accept an invitation to go somewhere with him. "I think he thinks we're dating but can't understand why I'm always busy," she says. "He just thinks I'm someone with a really full schedule because I rarely have time to see him."

Although she is beginning to understand that American men and Latin men view relationships with women differently, Pamela still forms friendships with guys, spends time with them, and gets confused when they mistake the exchange for dating. Derrick makes plans to go to an art exhibit with Pamela. He calls her three weeks beforehand because she always seems to be so busy. When the time rolls around to go to the exhibit, Pamela realizes she's not interested in spending the day with Derrick. So she cancels. "He has all these rules like 'Never cancel on a date,' so I know he's going to get mad," Pamela says. "But then he says that's what he likes about me—that I have my own mind."

Pamela knows Derrick is trying to date her and she knows she should tell him she's not interested, but she likes his company enough to be friends with him. So the next time he calls, she agrees to go out to dinner, knowing in the back of her mind that she'll probably end up canceling. She doesn't feel bad about stringing Derrick along because she doesn't think it's really her he likes so much as the idea of her. "He talks about me as though I am a decision he has made, and he's always congratulating himself on what a great choice I am," she says. Derrick tells Pamela he likes that she doesn't care if he valet-parks or not. "He didn't even ask me if I like men who like to save two dollars by not valet parking. He just assumes that I do. And to me, it's not worth a conversation to talk about the two dollars."

Pamela thinks Derrick views her as a good business decision. "He thinks, 'Okay, I have all these options, and let me choose one that suits me best.' But when you want a job, you may choose the one you think is best but you apply for many. You don't just decide one is the best and that's the job you're going to have without ever asking if they need anybody." Pamela finally tells Derrick she just wants to be friends. He stops calling her a couple of weeks later.

the daily mail

The remainder of my week follows a predictable pattern. I get some overly long, overly enthusiastic letters. I get some stock replies. I get a few terse hellos from people who invite me to view their profiles and to e-mail them if I'm interested. There are a few more winks and some nice, normal e-mails from people who sound like the kind of guys I'm friends with, the kind of people I like.

I get an e-mail from Charles. "Hi, ParisGal. I came across

your personal description while in search of a woman with whom I might mesh. The Internet is a clumsy tool at best and a poor substitute for real human interaction. Therefore, I propose that we meet to see if we might discover a mutual attraction. Will you join me for a pot of tea? If you read my profile and feel there might be reason to experiment with fate, please let me know. I shall wait to hear from you and if I don't, I shall wish you happiness."

The e-mails continue to filter in but in dwindling numbers. I hear from someone who just returned from Paris and loves the Grand Canyon. I am contacted by a man who has traveled to four dozen countries and loves his job as a veterinarian. I get a note from someone whose job takes him all over the world, including a few places I've never heard of. I look them up in an atlas. Each time I receive an e-mail, I look at the profile that goes with it. I can now see why it's nice to have a photo to go with a conversational style and a description. It's one more piece of a puzzle that can't possibly be completed in a virtual environment. The photos make the descriptions seem more real.

I write back to each man who contacted me and thank him for his note. I tell him I will be on the West Coast for the foreseeable future and will be taking my profile off the dating site. I don't want to lie. And I believe each of them deserves a response.

My final e-mail is from Travelguy99. "Hi, ParisGal. How are you? I never thought I'd find myself looking at Internet personals and really never imagined sending someone an e-mail. But you sound like the kind of person I get along with. Your profile reminds me of a lot of my friends. If my profile piques your interest, drop me a line. I'm always interested in meeting new people. Sincerely, Greg," he says, revealing his real name.

I remove my profile from the Match site and ask to discontinue my trial membership. This requires an exit interview by phone with a member of the Match staff who wants to know why I'm leaving and whether I am a satisfied customer. I tell him I'm in a relationship and no longer in need of the site's services. I become a statistic in the company's arsenal, proof that people are meeting and matching while using the site. I can't help thinking of the irony that the only time an actual human gets involved is when I'm ready to bid adieu.

freedom in anonymity

The Internet provides a chance to be an invisible participant, to test the waters of a new social scene, and to stay or go without anyone's noticing. It's anyone's fantasy of being able to be a fly on the wall at a party, to see who's there and what's happening without having to worry about saying the wrong thing to the man with the dirty martini or the woman with the poodle in her purse.

By the same token, however, virtual introductions, virtual dating, and virtual relationships deprive us of those very social challenges. It is the stuff of funny stories at best, horror stories at worst, when we make a grand social gaffe and live to tell about it. Planning out every word and phrase before hitting SEND does give us a measure of control, but it also deprives us of interactions that take place purely by chance. We have full freedom to ask for exactly what we want and to search for it among other profiles posted on a dating Web site. Dating then becomes an intellectual pursuit, rather than merely a physical one.

It is also probably the closest thing we have to old-fashioned courtship, a seeming paradox since we are more technologically advanced than ever. But online relationships return us to the days of the written word. They take us back to a time when people put careful thought into what they said to one another from the quiet privacy of a desk at home. Online correspondence returns us to the intimacy of crafting a near-perfect sentiment and sending it only when it conveys the proper emotion and meaning. And on the receiving end, we have the luxury of reading and rereading, infusing each word with the meaning we want it to have, separated from the sender by time and distance. We can indulge in a fantasy world where the person we imagine is not necessarily the person who would be sitting across from us over lobster dumplings with ponzu sauce.

Online dating is only one step in a relationship, however. There is something that remains in the realm of fantasy until two people meet in person. It doesn't even count to talk on the phone. The proof is in a real in-person date, same as it has always been. The only way to know for sure if there is any future with a prospective date is to meet in person. That is where the verbal sparring of e-mails or even the late-night pillow talk of phone calls become a person with three dimensions whom we are either attracted to or not. Otherwise, it's pure fantasy.

For his part, Dan goes back to the Internet and meets Lindy, who is bright, attractive, and within his target age range, which is several years younger than himself. They e-mail back and forth. Back and forth. After a month, Dan asks if Lindy would like to get together for a cup of coffee. She demurs, telling Dan she thinks he may be in a more serious relationship place than she is. "I only asked her to meet me for coffee, not to marry me," he says. "If she isn't interested in going on a date, what is she doing on a dating Web site e-mailing me for a month?"

Dan is fed up. He goes to a party where he only knows a couple of people. "Suddenly, I was faced with the old-school way we meet new people," says Dan. "And I had the strange sensation of looking around the room at the women and realizing I didn't know anything about them. I'd gotten so used to all my potential dates coming with a profile and a bunch of biographical information, that I didn't know what to make of live people I'd have to approach without knowing anything about them."

The profiles and searchable data can become a crutch. They can help us feel like we're stacking the odds in our favor when it finally comes time to go on a date. But if seeing it all on paper ahead of time ends up leaving us hamstrung when we actually have to introduce ourselves to a stranger at a party, is technology really moving us forward?

In San Francisco, the parade of blind dates begins to wear on Mimi. None of them is a good match and she doesn't want to waste her time going out on more than one or two dates before ending things. She begins to consider the formerly unthinkable: the Internet.

It's a generational thing, she says. "For people in their twenties, who were born into and grew up in a world of computers, Internet dating is just an adjunct to dating people they meet other ways. In our thirties there's nothing for Internet dating to be an adjunct to," Mimi says.

It's also a matter of pride. "It feels like I shouldn't have to go online to meet someone," she adds. "Yet I'm letting everyone set me up even if they haven't met the person. Putting my profile on-line feels like a job-application process. I'm a romantic, and the thought is so unappealing to me of saying, 'Here are my stats.'

"But in the end," she goes on to say, "if I met someone and fell madly in love, I'd have to wrinkle my brow to say we met online, but it would be well worthwhile to find someone I loved. And ul-timately I wouldn't care if that's how we met."

In inviting a lady to dance with you, the words, "Will you *honor* me with your hand for a quadrille?" or, "Shall I have the *honor* of dancing this set with you?" are used more now than "Shall I have the *pleasure?*" or, "Will you give me the *pleasure* of dancing with you?"

Offer a lady your arm and lead her to the quadrille, and in the pauses between the figures endeavor to make the duty of standing still less tiresome by pleasant conversation. Let the subjects be light, as you will be constantly interrupted by the figures in the dance. There is no occasion upon which a pleasant flow of small talk is more apropos and agreeable than in a ballroom.

FROM *The Gentlemen's Book of Etiquette, and Manual of Politeness,* BY CECIL B. HARTLEY, 1873

7.

the virtual date—
online chat

♥

♥

♥

It is the final frontier of remote dating: sitting at my computer, having a virtual conversation with someone I don't know—and if all goes well, someone I'll never know. Online chat rooms are the roadside truck stop of a new generation. Real names discouraged. Lying optional. Exaggeration essential.

Truthfully, I'm not sure if I'm ready for online chat. The one time I tried using a chat room previously was when I was working as a reporter. In an ill-conceived attempt to break a story on trends in hygiene, I began investigating a possible story about men wearing nail polish, à la Lenny Kravitz and other rock icons. Looking to find out if regular folk without recording contracts were in on the trend, I entered a chat room of thirtysomethings and posed a simple question, "Do any of you men wear nail polish?" My seemingly innocent query received a few sarcastic responses, and within seconds I was sent a message telling me I'd been unceremoniously booted from the room for trying to elicit lewd behavior. I never went back. The story about men's nail polish died as well.

So I can only imagine what I'm in for when I click the CHAT button on my AOL homepage. I decide to be a relatively passive participant at first. I choose a chat room called "On the beach" because it sounds fun and because it has thirty-six people in it. This means I can enter inconspicuously and see the kinds of things people are writing before I initiate any conversations. It turns out there's no such thing as passive participation. I immediately get an instant message from someone named hotgirl25, who writes, "How's everything?? That's a really nice screen name. I added you to my buddy list. So, I was wondering, what do you do for fun? Being a bad little girl is always fun. No? Hehe. Decide how bad I am from my PICS." I am not interested in hotgirl's pictures, nor do I want her e-mailing me every time I am online. I go to my instant-message controls and block her screen name from being able to contact me again.

I log out of that chat room and choose another, this one for "lesbians—40s" and watch the parade of abbreviated missives scroll their way up my screen.

"Lacylady, what do you drive?" asks Beenthere2.

"Whassup room?" Sally21 interjects.

"Anyone in Austin?" Cally7 asks.

"Nissan Sentra," Lacylady finally answers.

I decide to get bold. "How's it going, room?" I ask.

"Mine's a '79 Honda," Beenthere2 says, continuing the car talk with Lacylady. My query hangs out there. No one responds. It's like they can tell I'm a neophyte. Or maybe they hang out and chat with one another regularly and don't know me. And then there's the other possibility: that I am just a dork, ill-equipped for suave social interaction.

"I just got out of a relationship and I'm having a hard time meeting people," Chizzygal types.

"zzzzzz," is the response from more than one chat participant.

"Yeah, don't depress me," says Lacylady.

"LOL. Sorry," says Chizzygal. "Don't mean to be a downer."

I exit and log into "Singles Seeking Romance." Maybe I'll find a portal into twenty-first century dating here. But it's the same as the others. Within seconds an instant message pops up, asking if I want to have a private chat with Sexylegs7. I decline.

It turns out a lot of the people haunting chat rooms are all business, listing vital stats like age and location and entreating interested parties to send an e-mail. "Looking for a heavy guy? IM me," types HappySkeleton. "Fourteen years old, any California ladies wanna chat, IM me," says TeamXracer. And make no mistake, such one-on-one chat has a specific purpose: to pave the way for steamy virtual sex, or if two willing chatters are in the same city, for the real thing. A far cry from idle conversation, chat rooms are hookup venues, places to flaunt sexy pictures on Webcams, to invite each other into private randy conversations, or to solicit sex. When another chat room I visit settles into more banal banter between several of the participants, HandyHank complains, "These people don't want to hook up for sex. They just want to chat." He goes on to plug a "dating site" he found where people are "looking for more than just conversation." Chat rooms are the modern equivalent of looking for Mr. Goodbar.

Hooking up online has become a teen phenomenon, as evidenced by the number of chat-room participants who state their age as well below the statutory limit. The medium lends itself well to such encounters because it plays on teen commonalities: computers at the ready and urges to socialize at any hour, even if parents are in the next room. Raging hormones only add fuel to the fire.

This is not the first historical instance of casual encounters. In the 1930s and early 1940s, it was enviable to have lots of dates. Women were encouraged to be "once-arounders" at dances, taking turns with all the men in the room. Advice books cautioned against getting stuck for too long with one partner at a dance or swooning at the chance of a steady relationship: "Don't look overjoyed when a man dates you up. Take it as a matter of course. A man thinks he must be a sap if he is the only one who ever notices you. Act as if you could take 'em or leave 'em and it didn't matter which to you," says Dorothea Dix in 1939 in *How to Win and Hold a Husband*. Then the tides shifted in the 1950s, after World War II, when there was fear of a man shortage and a return to conservative times that valued going steady and marrying young. Today, we are on uncharted ground again, with technology making casual encounters possible between strangers and bridging the gap of loneliness. And while technology has historically brought couples closer together, today it also allows us to keep our distance and remain anonymous.

logging on and hooking up

"There are no last calls online," says Rick, who logs on to chat sites late at night after he comes home from the bar scene. "The regular scene gets tiring, trying to come up with the make-it-or-break-it pitch to get a girl's phone number. Online I can get up and leave a conversation and go back to it when I feel like it. With an in-person conversation, when you stall, you're dead," he says.

Rick bought a computer a few years ago, admittedly late to the e-mail game, and got hooked on what he could do from the privacy of his living room. "The AOL thing was a trip out of the grind—it stemmed from my desire not to go out on dates," he says. But he wasn't using online personals to find new dating prospects. He was using online chat rooms to have virtual dates via several hours of typed flirtation.

Chat rooms are an odd form of dating. For some people, they are a place to meet prospective dates in the hope that chats will evolve into in-person relationships. Indeed, chat relationships can lead to dates or even marriage. It's not so different from the days when women wrote to GIs during the world wars and hoped those on-paper relationships would evolve into real ones. And many of them did.

But there is another type of chat-room participant: people like Rick, who never intend to take anything further than late-night chat. For them the whole thrill is in talking anonymously and sharing jokes, intimate details, or even made-up descriptions from the safety of home, all the while knowing there's no chance of ever meeting in person. Not only can these virtual dates substitute for real ones, but in some cases they can be better, less aggravating, and more satisfying.

"Sometimes chatting felt better than what a real date would be," Rick says. Dates had started to feel like an interview process, loaded with questions about compatibility and fraught with pressure to squeeze a relationship from a so-so dinner conversation. "People around me are in terrible relationships. How could this not be a fun alternative?" he says.

Late at night, Rick would choose an AOL chat room and start a conversation with someone who had an intriguing screen name. "I'd pretend I was a guy in a cast who was in for the evening. I'd say I wanted to get frisky," he says. Chat rooms allowed Rick to hide the aspects of his life that he wished were different. No one would know if he was typing the truth because he'd never take his "dates" beyond the Internet.

back to the virtual trenches

I go back online and enter another chat room, hoping to see how this could possibly lead to dating success in any form. This time I choose a late-night hour, thinking the real surrogate for dating will more likely take place after the end of the workday. I log into the "Romance" section of AOL chat rooms and choose the "Christian singles" room. After about fifteen seconds of reading postings, it becomes clear that a rather heavy religious discussion is taking place. Trueblue4 writes, "God knows your capability, in spite of the situation." Yaweeh4 counters with "I think it is up to us to take the negativity and make it positive and to use it for God's purposes." And Megauni writes, "The great assurance we can have as Christians is that God is supremely sovereign, especially in our trials," only to be disputed by Igncorp, who says, "Not sure I agree with that one." In the midst of the discussion, Goodyally makes her own overture: "If there are any churchboys looking to chat with a churchgirl, just IM me." I log off.

I move on to "Alone at home" and find more of what I saw on earlier missions: invitations to view slutty pictures and requests for instant messages from anyone between the ages of fourteen and seventeen. And in "Hopeless Romantics," I find more of the same. Amid the entreaties to view Webcam shots, RacerDon88 asks, "Any girls from Wisconsin here?" I decide that the only way I'm going to understand what kinds of relationships can be born of chatting is to jump in. I post my own response: "I'm a Milwaukee gal."

Almost instantaneously, a little instant-message window pops open in the upper corner of my computer and RacerDon88 asks me my age. I wonder if he's hoping for a teenager or just making friendly conversation. I reply that I'm twenty-five, immediately understanding what's so insidious about meeting someone this way. I'm free to say whatever I want, to be whomever I want. And so is RacerDon88. The truth is, I only know what he tells me and I assume it to be true. Our chat ensues from there:

MyGirl61: Too old? Too young?

RacerDon88: no perfect age.

MyGirl61: guess that's true.

RacerDon88: i m 22. what part of wisconsin are you from?

MyGirl61: from nyc originally, making my way west. you from wisconsin? what part?

RacerDon88: yea im close to madison

MyGirl61: what are you doing chatting? there have to be some good reruns on . . .

RacerDon88: yea i guess. just looking to talk to someone. bored and lonely

MyGirl61: why lonely?

RacerDon88: no significant other

MyGirl61: friends to hang with?

RacerDon88: yea i have friends but i have work tomorrow

RacerDon88: what do you like to do

MyGirl61: tennis, backgammon, hiking

RacerDon88: cool.

MyGirl61: what do you like to do?

RacerDon88: drink. lift weights. hang out with friends

MyGirl61: did you go to school in the area?

RacerDon88: yea. i have one more year at college. i m home for the summer

MyGirl61: summer job? anything interesting?

RacerDon88: yea. working a retail job. video store, i love movies

MyGirl61: that's cool. do you get a discount?

RacerDon88: yea. it works out good

what do you do?

MyGirl61: grad school—economics.

RacerDon88: ouch. i barely passed my econ class at community college.

your a brave soul

MyGirl61: or crazy. where do you go to meet people there? good bars?

RacerDon88: i don't know. i am terrible at picking up people at bars

MyGirl61: no one's good at it.

RacerDon88: beer helps in a lot of ways. except driving

MyGirl61: don't drive.

RacerDon88: do you like to bar hop

MyGirl61: yep.

RacerDon88: nothing better then going out with friends, drinking, and not having to drive home.

MyGirl61: or work in the morning.

RacerDon88: yea. thats why they created sick days

MyGirl61: speaking of which, I have to be up early

RacerDon88: ok. hey can i put you on my buddy list

MyGirl61: sure

RacerDon88: my name is mike

MyGirl61: hi mike.

RacerDon88: cool i had fun talking to you

MyGirl61: you too. see ya.

And I go back to my life. It strikes me how many of us are isolated from a community of people whom we'd otherwise spend time with. But in many ways, the Internet provides that community. RacerDon and others like him do have a place to go at any hour of the day where they can find someone to talk to. RacerDon knows no more about me when we finish our chat than beforehand since I reinvented myself as a twenty-five-year-old economics student from Wisconsin who likes backgammon and barhopping. And the data he told me about himself could have been real or false. But in the end, when all we're looking for is some company, does it really matter?

"For centuries people met anonymously when they traveled and it was relatively free from consequences," says Malcolm R. Parks, who has done extensive research on personal relationships and social networks as professor of communication and Internet researcher at the University of Washington. "But if you and I are talking face-to-face and I say something flirtatious, you're right there, and like it or not, there will be some immediate response that is going to have consequences for me.

"I don't know," he goes on to say, "if we've ever had a medium that does it on this scale and does it interactively. Letter-writing and note-writing always allowed that same kind of disclosure, but what makes the Net different is that it's highly interactive. E-mail is not as interactive, but chat rooms and the like are real-time discussion venues. They stimulate a great deal of self-disclosure. People feel they've disclosed as much or more to each other than the friends they meet in person."

I suppose the next step in my budding online relationship, friendship or otherwise, would be for RacerDon to instant-message me the next time he sees that I'm online. And if we continued to get to know each other through chat and if I lived nearby in Wisconsin, we'd eventually meet. I wonder what the odds are of a romantic match between two strangers with time to kill at a similar hour and a common Internet service provider. I suppose they're as good as any.

part four

experts in the age
of information

Rob is single. The son of self-described hippie parents, Rob, twenty-five, was raised in a cabin in rural Virginia and moved after college to a small Kentucky town; population: 1,200. But Rob is not lonely. He runs a concert venue for underground music and is dating a woman he met through work. She lives four hours away in Harrisonburg, Virginia. Rob also does community radio work which sends him to New York every so often for conferences. He's dating Jen, a woman he met there who works for an independent radio charting company. He's also dating Mary, who goes to school three hours away and whose mom is Rob's neighbor. She introduced them because she didn't like Mary's previous boyfriend. "It's going to be interesting when she's in town and we go out and her mom is right there," Rob says. And there's Jeannie, who went to college with Rob. "We've been friends for six years and now it's blossoming into romance," he says.

For Rob, the challenge isn't in finding women open to dating. It's where to go on dates when the closest movie theater is a forty-minute drive away. "A lot of times it's just getting together at my house and me cooking or going to a park or going for a walk," Rob says. "If you want to go somewhere, it's a weekend trip." When Rob wanted to do something special for one of the women he's dating, he picked out a movie she'd been dying to see. But the closest theater where it was playing was in Knoxville—nine hours away. "If a girl is special, the trip is not a bad thing," he says.

People marry young in rural Kentucky, often right out of high school. Rob says he feels pressure to get into committed relationships in his rural community. "Family values and family ties are strong, and family is geographically here," Rob says. It's not uncommon to have several generations of a single family living in the same neighborhood. "I feel like the whole family is watching me to make sure I don't mess up and hurt their daughter or granddaughter's feelings," he says. There is a different set of pros and cons when it comes to new relationships. Because everyone has one or two degrees of separation, an aunt or a parent or a friend is always on hand to give Rob a firsthand screening of a potential date. On the flip side, it's tough to date someone without everyone in town knowing about the relationship.

Rob feels more pressure to get into a committed relationship living in Lexington than he did when he lived in Greensboro, North Carolina, where he went to college. He acknowledges that there are fewer people in rural communities, fewer activities, more of a desire for security. "I've tried to justify it as being part of the rural romantic life," Rob says. "Maybe people want relationships out of boredom. People don't get a lot out of sitting in their houses and reading so they want to be in relationships."

Rob admits that he's always overwhelmed in large cities like New York or Los Angeles. "I chalk it up to being used to a rural environment," Rob says. "Here I can be completely open and start talking to someone if I meet her in the grocery store." In large cities, Rob admits he is distracted by the abundance of choices and the overwhelming amount of stimuli. "I wonder if, in order to survive in an urban environment, it's necessary to give yourself some psychological blinders to focus on one path in life," he says. "I wonder, if I lived there, if I'd have to deaden some receptors to keep from being completely overwhelmed. It's like being in a video store with a kick-ass selection. It's really hard to pick one movie. But if it's a smaller video store with less abundance, you can find what you're looking for."

. . . [I]nstead of using the soul kiss, try what is known as the vacuum kiss. Here you start off by first opening your mouth a trifle just after you have been resting peacefully with closed lips. Indicate to your partner, by brushing her teeth with the tip of your tongue, that you wish for her to do likewise. The moment she responds, instead of caressing her mouth, suck inward as though you were trying to draw out the innards of an orange.

FROM *The Art of Kissing*, BY HUGH MORRIS, 1936

8.
dating in the age
of self-help:
the dating coach

After rooting around in singles events and online services, it occurs to me that maybe there's more to successful dating than merely finding new venues in which to meet people. Maybe the challenge lies in the dates themselves, the human interaction which will help us evaluate whether there is any potential for love. Maybe we've forgotten how to relate to each other.

In the world of modern dating conveniences, there are solutions for this as well: dating coaches who will analyze our dating flaws and for anywhere from $60 to $500 an hour, clue us in to better dating behavior.

I've heard that coaches can provide everything from advice on how to choose a hairstyle that says "date me" to wisdom on breaking down conversational barriers. I want the full gamut. I want someone to tell me not to wear a wristwatch because it makes me appear to be preoccupied with time or someone to tell me to sit forward in my seat to look like I'm engaged in the conversation. I want to know if my standard uniform of black pants, black sweater, and standout handbag is a smart, sophisticated choice or whether it just makes me look like I'm trying to hide fat hips. I want "date me" hair. And I want the ultimate elusive windfall: I want to know how to change my dating self in order to find love.

I am surprised that many of the dating coaches give advice only by phone. How can they tell whether I'm committing outfit faux pas if they can't see what I'm wearing?

listening for dating blunders

My first coach, a man named Barry with prominent ads on the Internet, tells me he can evaluate a person's dating roadblocks just fine over the phone, which is convenient because he's located in Chicago. He urges me to set up an appointment. We agree to talk for a half hour or so, during which time he tells me that he's spent thirty-three years working with singles, conducting what he calls psycho-education. "You may be asking what that means. It's a combination of psychology and education," he explains for the truly dim-witted.

Barry says that his particular brand of coaching is designed to get to the root of the behavioral processes which are standing in my way and change them so I can be a more productive dater. So far this sounds a lot like therapy. But he takes it a step further. He provides his clients with "skill sets broken down into steps" that will essentially give me a road map for my pursuit of love. Barry spins out all the pop-psychological buzzwords: emotional baggage, motivation, letting go. I get the impression I am about to be tricked into signing up for a lifetime of Freudian analysis, designed to enlighten me to the fact that all my issues with men relate back to my childhood.

I just want to know whether big hoop earrings make too big a statement and whether it's wiser to order a broad noodle in garlic sauce or just plain angel hair on the first date. Is sushi a bad idea? Too messy? Is broccoli rabe just an invitation to paranoia that something green is lodged between my teeth? Do I put people off with my tendency to sit back and evaluate rather than chattering through a catalog of information? How can I make my dating experiences more successful?

Barry begins with an "uptake session," designed to tell him what my dating needs are. This is hardly something I need to fabricate. It is the story of ten years of bad blind dates and my subsequently being labeled as "picky" by annoyed friends who refused to set me up on any more dates. I tell him it's hard to meet people I like because I have fairly high standards which few people meet in their entirety. The description also squares with much of what I heard in interviewing single men and women. No one wants to settle. We work hard; we lead interesting, full lives. We have involving careers and good friendships. Why should the person we're dating fall off the radar of acceptability?

I brace myself for Barry's reaction. I am certain he will tell me that high standards are just a euphemism for "picky," and that he will ship me off for expensive, long-term therapy. "Sometimes people's standards *are* too high," Barry says. As I suspected. "But I'd say ninety percent of the time, women's standards are *not* too high." Now I am intrigued. "I think women punish themselves when a relationship doesn't work out, thinking that they expected too much," Barry says. I want to know more about how he's formed this conclusion, but Barry lapses into lingo-laden double-speak once again.

"Your standards are directly proportional to your search strategy," he says. I have no idea what this means. He elaborates. It all comes down to endurance. "It's all about how many people you can meet in a lot of situations," he says. In other words, Barry is yet another proponent of dating as a chance to play the odds. I start to wonder if anyone outside the dating profession espouses the dartboard approach to dating: throw enough missiles at a target and a few are bound to hit. We all know it's hard to meet someone we're interested in dating long-term. Finding love is even more of a challenge. But love and romance are mystical intangible concepts. It's hard to equate them with trawling for schools of fish rather than hanging a single lure.

Then I talk to Cameron, forty-five, who does think of dating as a statistical pursuit. "If you draw a series of five concentric circles, the fifth ring is the total contact potential in your dating lifetime that you can meet," he says. "Then the fourth ring is your dating universe, the ones you'd actually date. The third ring is the individuals you'd date who have some potential. The second is the ones with the greatest potential, and the innermost circle is 'the one,' the nirvana of dating."

Cameron lives in Portland, Maine, not too far from the coastal town of Belfast where he grew up, but a world away from the small-town life some of his old friends have continued to lead in the town with population 6,500. Many of Cameron's friends married right out of college, something Cameron finds a bit suspicious, given the small sample size they had to choose from. "When I look at my friends in small towns who seem happy being married to their high school sweethearts, I have to ask whether they were just lucky to run into 'the one' early on or whether there's just a desire to be married," Cameron says. "Our grandparents never went outside five square blocks from their neighborhoods, and they met and married. What does that tell you?"

But in some ways, Cameron concedes, it's easier when the numbers are smaller, the choices fewer. "If you like jazz music, you could have a venue with twenty things to do on any given weekend. Your choice is much easier if you only have one or two options," Cameron says. "You tend to work harder at it if there are fewer choices. Rather than thinking there is greener grass or blonder hair around the corner, just look at what's in front of you."

Despite the fact that he's moved from city to city across the country, working for various technology companies, Cameron has never had trouble meeting people. He's used the Internet, he's gone to singles clubs, attended dances, and asked friends to set him up. "People who say it's hard to meet are the ones who don't allow themselves the opportunity. You're not going to meet someone if you stay home every weekend," Cameron says. All the same, Cameron concedes that quantity isn't always the answer. "We have access to so many people that it's almost too many choices. The ease of access makes it easier to meet but harder to match."

The larger the city Cameron has lived in, however, the more people he has had to meet in order to find dates that approach his inner circle. Cameron has used matchmaking services and attended dinner parties with ten single friends, each of whom had to bring another single friend. Ultimately, he met the woman he's now dating through friends on the West Coast who thought the two might get along. "It's a pure numbers game. The chances of finding the top one hundred best matches for you is largely dependent on the exposure you have to the world," Cameron says. Barry would be proud. Or so I think.

Barry says he is loath to think of dating solely in terms of raw numbers because that simplifies things too much. The answer isn't merely meeting lots of people because that's not realistic: most of us don't have the endurance required to sift though all the wrong people required to ferret out the right ones. "Some people only have the emotional endurance to handle forty people instead of three hundred," he says. "And for some of us, our work and sleep schedule is such that we can't meet more than forty."

True, there are only so many times we can play hooky from work to look for love at the mall. And sacrificing sleep for the sake of another five lackluster dates is rarely the answer. I'm hoping Barry can provide a bit more targeted advice.

barry wants details

I tell Barry a bit more about my life, basically describing my outlook during the endless black hole of my dating years and building a composite from the single people I've interviewed. I tell him

I have a good job in a field I like. It's not interesting to me to go out with someone who hates his job and is looking for someone to live vicariously through. I tell him I have lots of great friends and plenty of activities. In truth, most of the people I meet and talk with have very active, interesting lives; good friends; strong careers. They are looking for someone who matches these attributes. Their dating lives may be the one area where they haven't been able to hit a home run.

Barry tells me I remind him a lot of himself.

He, too, loves his career and has spent a long time working to be able to do what he loves. He tells me he dated a string of women during his twenties, many of them students in his relationship seminars. Then he met the woman whom he'd later marry. They moved in together when he was twenty-nine and got married six years later. "I thought I was commitment-phobic," he confides. "And it was something I was able to work through by talking to other people about their relationship problems." He tells me it's very common in his profession to be able to help others while dealing with your own issues.

Dating coach, coach thyself.

Barry can relate to me, he says, because he, too, has always had high standards. And he doesn't think there's anything wrong with that. "You and I are a special breed and it's hard to find someone who measures up," he says. I start to understand the method Barry used to elicit dates from his patients.

But, he says, "I think you would benefit from finding some new friends, people who stimulate you." We haven't talked at all about my friends, who are actually just fine.

Barry doesn't urge me to lower my standards, but he does warn

me that I may become so set in my ways that I may pass up the
window of opportunity for finding romance, especially considering my age. I have passed the scary threshold into my midthirties.

He wants to know how many long-term relationships I've had.
I tell him two—one that lasted for three years, the other a year.
He chuckles when I refer to the one-year boyfriend as a relationship. "I meant long-term," he says. I tell him that I consider a year
to be a pretty long term, especially when it's tough to find someone I like enough to endure three dates. "Fair enough," he says.

"So, playing devil's advocate, what would you say to someone
who asked you why you've only had two long-term relationships
by age thirty-five?"

"First of all," I tell him, "I've had a lot of dates, a lot of three-
month relationships over the years. I have been busy. Second, I
think two long-term relationships is pretty good by age thirty-five."

"Very good, good answer," Barry says. "I agree with you." I
start to wonder if Barry's version of coaching is simply to tell me
I'm doing everything right and send me on my way.

I have to ask what he intends to talk to me about if I agree to a
lengthy coaching session. "We'd talk about some strategies you
could use to meet more people," he says.

"So, for example, might your advice be that I should sign up
with an online dating service?"

"That might come up," he admits. "Or we could come up with
other places where you might meet people," he says.

I start to wonder why I would pay someone to help me dream
up places to go where there might be single people. I have to
imagine that anyone who has been dating for a while would have
run the gamut: signed up for the art classes where "I will just be

enriching myself but where I might meet a like-minded budding artist." Or let friends and coworkers know I'd be open to being set up on a date.

He says we would talk about my experience with these various venues and my "personal roadblocks" that are preventing me from finding a date I can live with—or at least someone I can stand to look at for a meal of two courses or more.

I can see that if I am merely in need of a pep talk to get myself out the door, I might be able to work with Barry on overcoming my fears and putting myself out there. But given that I just want to know what I may be doing wrong on a date and how to meet the "right" people more successfully, something everyone who is single would like to know, Barry's advice in this area doesn't seem worth paying for.

On the contrary, he tells me, "You sound very well-adjusted. You could probably teach me a few things."

moving on

Barry is not the solution to my coaching needs. I suppose he might be the solution for some people, but only if they are more confused than he is.

I still want to know if there are purported experts out there who will sit me down and tell me what kind of image I'm putting out there for a prospective date and what kind of solutions they can provide for any of my conversational or grooming blunders that are standing between me and love.

I put in a call to Rhonda, whose Internet ad boasts that she has helped people around the world, appeared on TV, and been inter-viewed about her techniques in numerous publications. Rhonda's voice mail is cheery and upbeat, urging me to leave her a list of times when I can be reached so we don't play phone tag. She doesn't want to waste any time.

"What seems to be going on?" Rhonda asks when we do make contact. After my conversation with Barry, I want to avoid any in-vitation to the pursuit of psycho-education.

I tell her I am not looking for a therapist. I am just looking for someone who can tell me if I'm putting out a good vibe on a date. I tell her that people have told me I am sometimes hard to read, in-timidating even. She says she has just the right thing for someone like me.

"I know what men are thinking," she says. "And that's why I can help you." Rhonda, who calls herself the Sweetheart Surgeon, tells me she has been trying to train her male clients to understand powerful women. "They're not used to listening," she says. I'm reminded of my golden retriever who has the same problem.

Rhonda fills me in on the kinds of things she can help me with for $150 per hour. There will be wardrobe consultations. She will take me shopping for clothes that aren't too dowdy, if that turns out to be my problem. We will talk about the kind of energy I project without even knowing it. She'll visit my house and tell me whether I'm living the kind of life of someone who is ready for love.

Rhonda says she will make me aware whether the words I use are turning people on or off. "It's unconscious," she says. "They come from old fears and bad relationships." Rhonda admits that she herself went to therapy to deal with just these types of issues.

"I was on this quest. I had issues myself of not wanting to look too sexy, or not wanting to look too frumpy." The time Rhonda spent working out her issues made her realize how much she could help other people with their concerns. It is a familiar refrain among the league of "experts."

We talk some more, and Rhonda tells me that it doesn't matter where my issues originated. Besides, Rhonda surmises, it was probably just the father who was a control figure or the passive-aggressive mother. Everyone has these problems. But it's all part of the past. She is not interested in putting me on the couch to figure out why. She'd rather look forward. Her coaching is all about achieving goals quickly. "You can create whatever you want," she says.

help me, rhonda

Rhonda promises that I, too, can learn her secrets. Some of what we'll work on is making sure I wear feminine clothes to make men notice me. She'll even teach me how to flirt.

"There are visual, emotional, and verbal ways to attract a man," Rhonda says. "It's not just about wearing a sexy top that shows your boobs." I breathe a sigh of relief for intelligent women everywhere.

Then Rhonda continues: "It's about showing your boobs combined with other things."

Rhonda suggests that we meet at my house. She wants to check out my wardrobe, see what she can tell about me from where I live. Several thoughts run through my head. I consider asking a single friend if I can borrow her apartment for the morning so Rhonda can evaluate me in the natural environment of a single woman. I consider inviting her to my own house and closing the door to my son's room and attempting to scrub the place of all traces of one-year-old. I figure I will have to keep her out of my husband's closet and explain why I have so much stuff. I consider telling her my apartment is being fumigated for an indefinite period and I'm house-sitting for married friends. It is amazing how many thoughts rush through my head in the span of thirty seconds while Rhonda is telling me why it will be so great for her to see where I live.

Ultimately, none of my concocted scenarios seems like the right solution when my objective is to have her evaluate me, a woman she's never met, who has difficulty putting on the right face with a man.

I suggest instead that we meet at a bar or coffeehouse, the kind of places where a first date might take place. If she wants to evaluate the single version of me in my natural habitat, she needs to visualize me on a date.

Rhonda leaves me to check my schedule to figure out when I'm free to meet for our first session. I promise to call her in a few days. "And cheer up!" she says, almost whispering like a conspiratorial schoolgirl hatching a plan to get the football quarterback to notice the plain, brainy girl. "I'll teach you everything you need to know."

two weeks later

I walk into the coffee bar where Rhonda and I agree to meet, looking for a woman who resembles the photo on her Web site. I am not surprised to find that Rhonda is more heavily made-up, a little older, and a little plainer than the photo. She shakes my hand and looks me up and down, giving no obvious sense of approval or worry.

We sit. Rhonda puts on a big friendly smile, acting almost giddy, like this will be a fun-filled hour of girl talk and exciting new revelations for me. She has an array of tea-drinking paraphernalia in front of her—metal water pot, honey packets, spoons, napkins, and tea bags—and a yellow legal pad and a stack of papers. It all looks very official and promising.

I take a good look at the woman who supposedly holds the secrets to successful dating. She appears to be about fifty, trying to look younger. Her red, highlighted hair is partially pulled up into a clip with a girlish fringe of bangs dancing across her brow. She has a heavy swath of dark eyeliner painted around her eyes and a ten-minute application of mascara. There's an oval of pinkish blush swept up along each cheek. Rhonda tends to oversmile, revealing a big row of polished teeth behind brownish-pink lipstick.

Her black T-shirt is cut in a deep V-neck which accentuates some cleavage and her tanned arms. Black pants don't do enough to hide figure flaws below the waist but she compensates with a distracting silver hip-hugging belt with a big flower buckle.

Rhonda inventories my "look." She tells me I could do with some mascara to make my eyes "pop." She looks me over and says that, like her, I "don't have too much on top." Nevertheless, I should "sex it up" a bit with a cleavage-baring top of my own. And she says I need to smile. "It will light up your face and you need that," she says. Rhonda takes in my stock outfit of white T-shirt and black pants and tells me there needs to be something conversational about my outfit—an accessory men will notice.

I don't know how many men Rhonda actually knows, but the ones I am friends with live in fear of appearing too knowledgeable about women's accessories.

"Tell me what brought you here," Rhonda says.

I explain that it's not so much that dates are hard to come by as the fact that it's hard to make a real connection. I'm wondering if it's me. Maybe there's something I'm putting out there as an independent woman with a career that is giving off the vibe that I don't want a relationship.

Rhonda starts nodding her head as though she knows what my problem is. "Men need three or four good signs that you're interested. Their egos are huge," she tells me, in a woman-to-woman, knowing tone. In a replay of our earlier telephone conversation, Rhonda says that successful men aren't used to powerful women. On the contrary, *they* need to be made to feel powerful and special. They need me to reinforce that they are amazing. "Then they will reward you and take you out to nice places and buy you things," she says. I said I was looking for a connection—not an expense account. Rhonda tsk-tsks that notion. I need to play into the stereotype of a fawning, submissive woman so my man can tromp home with a new bauble each night. The thought makes me wince.

Rhonda takes my hand across the table and tells me she can relate. "I know, it pisses us off to have to say those words, but you have to give men obvious signals." Apparently, I have to bat my eyes adoringly and tell men they are big and manly. Absolutely, says Rhonda: "Men are confused by strong, intelligent women. It is our job to make them think we are the weak, dim-witted fawns they can relate to. I hear my inner Eleanor Roosevelt cringing.

It's just an issue of genetics, Rhonda tells me: "Men are eighty-five percent visual. They're all about animal attraction."

"Do you really think I should give up my principles and just push my breasts in men's faces?" I ask.

"It couldn't hurt," she says.

i'm no casanova

After sitting with me for fifteen minutes, Rhonda concludes that I am putting out a vibe that says I am prissy and standoffish. "Do you like to have fun? Do you actually think of yourself as a fun person?" she asks, not bothering to hide the doubt in her voice. I start feeling defensive. Even though I am paying Rhonda for objective criticism, I recoil at the thought that she may be right. Prissy? No one has ever used that word to describe me. At least not to my face. But I look down at my conservative choice of outfit and think about the last time I wore the punch bowl at a party. Immediately my confidence is stripped bare. Maybe I've been kidding myself all these years, thinking I'm adept in social situations. Maybe I am the cardigan-sweatered librarian of the dating world. Meanwhile, I've been going along picturing myself as a cocktail waitress in a tube top.

Fear not, Rhonda says. She can help me correct my prim, un-savory ways, using the teachings of neurolinguistic program-ming. I have no idea what this is. Suddenly we've left the realm of dating and launched deep into self-help terminology. Heaven help me if I've inadvertently wandered into some kind of cult.

Rhonda tells me that somewhere in between dropping out of college and taking courses in psychology and religion, she found her true beliefs in the field of neurolinguistic programming. Rhonda spends an expensive ten minutes explaining the underpin-nings of the faux science, using terms like "patterns," "implanting thoughts," and "mental tape recorder." In a nutshell, Rhonda's school of thought falls under the heading of self-fulfilling prophecy. We start to believe anything we say enough times, whether it's positive or negative. The trick, Rhonda says, "is to delete the neg-ative thoughts from the computer in your mind and replace them with what you want in life."

I have heard this before. Some of us chant or meditate about the things we want. Others pray. And some of us just call it "drive and focus." Rhonda—and apparently others—call it "neurolin-guistic programming."

Rhonda tells me I should help program the people around me to understand what I'm looking for in a relationship by telling them over and over again. And I should program the computer in my head. Instead I try to reprogram the direction of our conver-sation. I think I was happier with "cleavage" and "prissy."

rhonda's love life at
$2.50 a minute

Rhonda tells me she has never been married and only recently has met a man she's consistently dating. It begs the obvious question: isn't it hard to give out advice on finding the right romantic match when you yourself are single? Rhonda pooh-poohs this notion, saying that the fact that she has spent so many years preparing herself to meet the right romantic match actually makes her quite an expert on the subject. She fills me in on her own boyfriend quest, which was just satisfied a year ago.

"You never know when you're going to meet your soul mate, so you have to be ready," Rhonda says. She got ready by buying the kind of sheets she imagined sleeping on with her ideal boyfriend and stocking up on sexy lingerie and the type of underwear she'd want a man to see. Rhonda tells me she replaced pictures of Botticelli women on her walls with a photograph of a brawny sailor rescuing a mermaid. "That was my fantasy and I wanted to see that message every day."

Rhonda tells me I need to lie in bed each night and imagine the man I want to be with, imagine what it would be like to be married. She says that if I can successfully give off the vibe that I am already in love, I will be irresistible to men because they will be attracted to that vibe. I am not supposed to worry if everyone thinks I am crazy, she says: "Friends of mine used to say, 'Who is he? You're acting like you're in love, who's the guy?' And I'd tell them, 'I haven't met him yet, but he's amazing.'"

Rhonda is a cheerleader. Her goal is to motivate and inspire.

She is a coach not unlike the soccer coaches I had as a kid who told me to speed toward the goal line and kick the hell out of the ball. Rhonda is essentially telling me the same about dating.

Rhonda coaches both women and men, but she takes a particular interest in the dating tribulations of men because "as a woman, I know what men want," she says. To that end, Rhonda has written and self-published a book, giving men a step-by-step regimen for tackling dating blunders. A lot of her advice is the same as what she's telling me: "Act as if" you already have what you want and you'll be able to attain it—make your home ready for love. But the book goes a step further, giving men specific pointers on dress and grooming. They're told that deodorant is crucial and that women like the soft skin that results from using body lotions and oils. Men are clued in to the effect of a sharp wardrobe with accessories like "tasteful jewelry," matching belts and shoes, and a cell phone with a distinctive ring. Bad breath and stained teeth are a no-no.

After the chapters on clothing and hygiene fix-its, Rhonda returns to the mantra of self-actualization. And sure enough, three-quarters of the way in, she lets men in on the virtues of neurolinguistic programming. I am relieved. I was beginning to fear she'd forgotten about reprogramming men's mental computers, what with all the talk about arranging fresh flowers around the house and keeping their sex drives alive with nutritional supplements. In the final chapters, Rhonda reemphasizes the importance of self-love and gives men a last vote of encouragement: believe in love and it will come.

How different is Rhonda's brand of coaching from the advice of a doting mother who tells her son to wear a bit of cologne or a nice sweater when he goes out on a date? How different is Rhonda's think-positive song from the mantra of so many other self-help gurus who are in business to boost our egos and get us to feel better about ourselves?

We talk some more about Rhonda's quest for the right romantic partner. She tells me she was dating a man who seemed like a good prospect. He was sweet and caring, and she was starting to think the relationship would turn into something. Then she found out he was married with three kids. "It turned out he was separated but still living with his wife," Rhonda says, adding that she thinks he avoided telling her about the family because he knew she was a dating coach. The nonexperts usually take such news in stride.

She broke up with the man shortly thereafter. "I lay in my bed that night and said, God, I know you have a plan for me. I don't know what it is, but I'm waiting to find out."

Rhonda was still hopeful that the right guy was out there, waiting for her to find him. She went back to her college town for a wedding and got set up on a blind date. He seemed too good to be true. He had a ranch, a collection of cars, and a big house—all things he assumed were important to Rhonda. But she began to grow tired of his boastful descriptions of his lifestyle accoutrements and ultimately broke off the date after a half hour. "I just felt like our values were different," she says.

Instead of pursuing the blind date, Rhonda opted to head out with friends to a local bar. They didn't want to go, but she dragged them anyway—just for one drink. "We got to the bar and I stood in the middle, in a noticeable spot," Rhonda says. There she bumped into a man who went to another college in the area. "He just happened to be there for a family reunion that weekend," she says. They started talking and Rhonda really liked him. She was hesitant to date someone who lived in a different city, but before long his job transferred him closer by. They've been dating for eight months.

"I just knew if I asked for the kind of man I wanted that I'd end up finding him," Rhonda says. She immediately sat her boyfriend down and described what she was looking for in a relationship. "I told him I wanted someone who would enhance my life, fulfill my fantasies, and create a great romantic life," she says.

Rhonda confides that her boyfriend is a great guy and that she makes him feel amazing. "I know the right things to say to make him feel empowered. If he gets cocky, I pull back a little bit and he comes running. Just like a little dog." She continues. Dating successfully is all about using the right words to make men feel empowered, Rhonda says. "So many women wonder why smart men are with bimbos. Well, that bimbo made him feel smart and empowered and amazing."

I look at my watch and realize we've been talking about Rhonda's love life for the past thirty minutes.

rhonda digs deeper

We continue talking about patterns that I've put into the computer in my mind. Rhonda is convinced that something in my past brainwashed me into thinking I'd get hurt if I tried to love another person. She throws out some possibilities: my father, my mother, a past boyfriend. "If you think you're not going to have love, that idea gets implanted," she warns. Rhonda tells me to delete the negative tape recording in my mind. She tells me to think positive thoughts. She tells me to meditate. I mentally vow to get up right now if she references the deep thoughts of Jack Handey.

It's not all about visualizing the perfect boyfriend, Rhonda says. Sometimes it's just about attracting a fill-in boyfriend. If the right guy doesn't come along, there's no reason I can't have fun. Rhonda says I should indulge in a self-caring routine that includes frequent massages and lovers on the side. And I should wear midriff-baring tops if I want to attract some attention. "Men love to see a little skin," she says. In fact, she adds, I should dress every day as though I were on a date. Right down to the underwear. "If you were going out with a guy, you'd wear nice underwear, just in case he ended up seeing it," she says with a wink.

But she has a strong word of caution: "Casual sex is fine but don't let your in-between man take up too much space in your life." Rhonda's fear is that having a lover on the side will be so satisfying that I will stop using my mental energy to search for a permanent actor to fill the role.

From across the table, I can smell Rhonda's perfume, which has a strong patchouli scent. I wonder if she will advise me to wear perfume in order to be more appealing to the male nose.

Overall, it's just an issue of using my "spiritual powers," Rhonda tells me. Most people have negative thoughts 70 percent of the time, she says. Her goal for me is to have positive thoughts 70 percent of the time. That way, I will be in control of my fate. "I am certain that there is somebody out there for you," she says.

"I hope so," I tell her, just like anyone would in the same situation. "No," Rhonda says. "That's your problem. You can't *hope*. You have to be *certain*." And we're back to the mantra of visualizing what I want in order to get it.

where to meet men

It turns out I have been going to all the wrong places in my search for a date. Since Rhonda met her current boyfriend in a bar, she knows from experience that bars are a good place to meet men. She tells me to think about the kinds of places that make me feel most comfortable, most beautiful. I'm not sure I'm likely to meet men at a day spa and even the bars I know of with decent lighting are a far cry from making me feel beautiful.

Of course, there's no guarantee that the men I'll meet in a bar will appeal to me, Rhonda says. Especially, she says, because 80 percent of people don't like the careers they've chosen and are likely to come across as bitter and depressed. Rhonda can tell that these types of men will not appeal to me because I like my career— just like the other 20 percent of the population. And coincidentally, like Rhonda herself. She has another suggestion for meeting men: something called the Millionaires Club.

I can't imagine that separating men out according to net worth is really the answer to kinship. I ask her if she has any other suggestions. I am not asking for men with money—just intelligence. I see a little lightbulb flash behind her mascara-laden eyes: "You might want to sign up for some neurolinguistic programming classes."

Rhonda certainly seems to be the victim of some kind of programming. She has a one-track mind and a set repository of answers for the questions she anticipates. It reminds me of the old standby method of studying for a history exam by memorizing a few facts and dates and working them into the answer of whatever essay question is asked. My personal favorite was to mention the McCormick reaper and the combine thresher in any American history essay about the Industrial Revolution. But for $150 an hour, I do not want Rhonda's CliffsNotes version of relationship advice.

on the date itself

Now it's time to talk about the impression I make on an actual date. Not only am I supposed to pretty myself up with a little makeup and cleavage à la Bourbon Street, I am supposed to reach across the table and touch the man I am on a date with. This will give him a subtle signal.

For the twenty-first century, this advice is awfully provincial. Maybe we have moved so far into the future that we are actually just repeating the past. It begins to infuriate me that Rhonda and others like her are putting themselves out as experts, collecting our hard-earned money and giving us little that we didn't know in the first place. I am sickened that our economy supports anyone with a whim of an idea and the gall to charge a fee for sharing it. Some services should not be paid for, no matter how busy we are.

But I barely have time to consider this, lest I miss Rhonda's next salient bit of advice. She goes on: the conversation I have on a date is key to determining if I'm with my ideal man. Rhonda doesn't trust me to know how to recognize a guy with romantic potential so she feeds me a few prompter questions to help me distinguish him from the ravioli appetizer I'm apt to be having.

"You need to figure out what you value and ask questions to figure out if he has those values, too," she says. Then she sits back and smiles, as if to let the words wash over me a second time. I can't imagine how many people would sit through dinner with a date and avoid asking any questions that might reveal whether they had anything in common with the person across the table. Rhonda must think her clients lack the basic skills of human interaction.

"Are there certain types of conversational topics that you think should be off-limits when talking to men for the first time?" I ask. Maybe I am getting too serious, too soon, talking about work and life passions on a first date. Rhonda thinks there's something to this. Men, she says, do not like a woman to be too intense and involved in work. "That's where they expect to excel. They want to talk about their fabulous jobs. You just need to be fabulous and men will love you," she says.

Never should there be analytical queries posed on a date. I am supposed to be surreptitious in my questioning, in order to elicit the information I need without making the man across the table feel as though I am asking anything at all. "That is how women get the upper hand," Rhonda says.

I ask Rhonda if she's sure she isn't setting me up for a very outmoded if not stereotypical relationship with man as career-oriented provider and woman as fabulous, doting sidekick. She says that's not the point. I need to stop confusing the men I meet. "You want a man to come in and enhance your life. You're not looking for someone to sweep you off your feet—you want some-one to be proud of what you've accomplished," Rhonda says. "Men don't understand that."

First off, given that I know men and count many of them as close friends, I have a hard time believing this is true. Second, if it's somehow true that men really don't understand, why not edu-cate them? Again Rhonda tells me I'm missing the point.

In fact, I think I see it quite clearly.

god help me, rhonda

What makes this woman an expert? In our service economy, is any-one who has had experiences automatically an expert? Since when did having everyday experiences like having our hearts broken or searching unsuccessfully for love qualify us as good teachers?

Of course, it is comforting to think that there are people out there who know more than we do. We hope there are profession-als who can give us the answers we seek. They are out there with an ad in a magazine, an appearance on a talk show, or a shingle on the Internet. And they are proffering a solution to our dating woes. For a hefty fee. But are they experts at anything other than savvy marketing and the accrual of quick cash?

In order to find anything of value in the innumerable services available to single adults, we have to become experts ourselves. We have to learn to read between the lines of slick advertising. Is someone who has a "surefire technique" really just spouting off truisms learned in a touchy-feely seminar? Or is the expert really just an ordinary adult who has learned a few life lessons on the way to a relationship and who now believes those lessons comprise a new doctrine? Do we really need advice from experts?

Anyone with eyes could critique my choice of clothes. Any stranger could tell me what kind of first impression I make. Maybe they'd call me prissy or maybe they'd choose some other adjective.

Rhonda writes "home study" notes for me on a yellow legal pad, using a blue calligraphy pen, scrawling her notes across the page in loopy script. A flirty, feminine type of writing that she'd probably tell me to adopt as a way to attract men. I can hear it now, "Practice writing the type of love letters you'd like to receive from *him*." She plans to send me home with some key questions to ponder and some "homework." I read some of the questions upside down as she writes them: "Can you see yourself in a real relationship?" "What is your ideal?"

The more we talk, the more I start to become shocked that I ever found relationships at all in my thirty-plus years. I never spent my nights lying in bed, dreaming of the characteristics of the man I would be searching for the next day. I never made over my apartment with sheets designed for the perfect romantic night or proper mood-lighting in case the right guy happened into my life. And there were never perfect panties. Are all these techniques really necessary? Or were they just necessary for Rhonda?

We talk for a few more minutes about how I can speak, using words that empower my vision for my future relationship. Then I call it a proverbial night.

I write Rhonda a check for $225 for an hour and a half. She offers to spring for the cup of coffee I drank during our time together. It would be hard to feel like I got enough out of the session to consider my money well spent. And the prospect of meeting again to get additional expensive tips doesn't seem worthwhile.

Whether it's someone telling me to send mental hugs to the man across the room or advising me to picture the perfect man in my head so I can envision finding him, the message is really the same. These "professionals" are in the business of making us feel better about where we are in life, whether we end up meeting someone or not. And they do it for a price. Many of the dating "experts" trade on the ability to jump-start us into action. It almost doesn't matter what kind of action. We could turn around after a seminar or a coaching session and post an online profile or ask our next-door neighbor out for coffee. The point is just to get us to do something.

They are the dating equivalent of a Weight Watchers meeting. They hold us accountable for making change in our own dating lives by getting in our faces and cheering for us. If we leave even a little bit inspired to smile a little brighter at the next person we find attractive, they feel they've done their jobs. And maybe they have.

Rhonda walks me to the door of the coffee shop and gives me a hug. "You're gonna do just fine," she says with a big smile, sending me out into the world.

Her perfume hangs on my clothes for the rest of the day.

the follow-up

Rhonda calls me the next day on my cell phone. She wants to know how I am. "I feel like we really connected," she tells me. I am at work. I am busy. Our session of girlish chitchat is over. And I don't really want to pay more money to listen to Rhonda try to sell me on matchmaking services, the speed-dating events she hosts, or more sessions designed to make over my dating self. "Do you feel inspired?" she wants to know.

"I do, I feel inspired," I lie, knowing it's what she wants to hear. Rhonda sounds satisfied, almost gleeful. I can feel her winking on the other end of the line, like we're sisters sharing intimate details about our love lives. I hang up the phone and move on to the next set of experts.

"She is very deep; you will find her worth cultivating," was said to me once of an "unapproachable" woman whose "keep-off-the-grass" attitude had repelled me at first meeting.

I devoted myself to a search for her hidden worth; but after many months I found her to be like one of those sterile New England farmlets where a fresh crop of stones appears as soon as the old ones are uprooted. Who does not recall a pounded thumb and wasted temper in his youth, trying to break the shell of a tough walnut, only to find a dried and shriveled meat within?

FROM *Men, Women and Emotions,* BY ELLA WHEELER WILCOX, 1898

9.

san francisco and the virtual singles seminar

In a noodle shop near the San Francisco Embarcadero, Emily special-orders a bowl of whole-wheat soba with broccoli and very little sauce. She picked the restaurant. She always picks the restaurant, she says. It's the first rule of dating for picky eaters, designed to make sure the evening doesn't get off to a rocky start because her date chooses a restaurant where she won't like the food.

But at the moment, that's the least of Emily's concerns about her dating life. "I don't feel romantic when I go out at the end of a workday. Everyone drives me crazy at work, and I don't want to have to motivate to be in a good mood to meet someone new," says Emily, a thirty-two-year-old, high-level manager for a large clothing maker in San Francisco. These days she's having a hard time mustering up the energy to go on dates at all. "Corporate America leaves you emotionally drained and beat-up at the end of the day," she says. Emily spends her days managing a staff of employees and overseeing budgets and meetings. The hours are long. There's little time for much else. Emily's free time is divided between fitting in a workout at the gym, seeing friends, or taking a chance on a blind date. "All my energy goes into managing people. I'm giving all my love to them—there's nothing left over for a date."

When Emily sits down for dinner with Steve, a complete stranger introduced by a friend, it's hard to muster the energy to put on a good show. And a show is necessary because Steve is busy, too, and he isn't going to date her a second time if she seems uptight and obsessed with work. Emily and Steve make it through dinner and part ways. It's an ordinary date, nothing special. They probably won't go out again. "We make it hard for ourselves. We choose these hard-core careers, and then we don't have time or energy to spend on our personal lives," says Emily. Sometimes it's easier not to date at all. "But when I just put blinders on and move forward with work, weeks slide away, and then months," she adds.

Across town in a bar near the Marina, George echoes the dating-derailed-by-work anthem. "When you're single, you work hard by default. There's no family you need to go home to," says George, a well-dressed, good-looking blond man who has lived in cities around the world. What's more, work can serve as a convenient excuse: if he has nothing going on in his social life, he can pour all of his energy into his career and convince himself that he could be dating if not for the demands of his job at a technology company. "Work seems to be the single person's relationship," he says. "I can stay late when other people have to go home to their families. When you're single, it's easy to just work really hard and forget about doing anything else." But that's a temporary solution. "I want a woman in my life. I want to have kids," he says. "I don't want work to be everything."

In the dozen years since he graduated from college, George never spent much time worrying about his dating life. He always met women, either through friends or at bars or just in the neighborhood. But suddenly, at age thirty-four, he's finding that his dating pool has run dry. He rarely meets women at work, he's not interested in trolling the bars, and his apartment in a suburb of San Francisco takes him out of the social scene physically. "I don't know how I went from having a social life to sitting around my house on a Friday night, trying to divine ways to meet a woman," he says. "And that's the difference now. I don't want to just date. I want to meet someone."

Jody, also a San Francisco resident, is a smart, successful business-school graduate who shares the desire to meet someone. But it's not easy. "First impressions are really hard," Jody says. "I don't come across the way I am once someone gets to know me. I'm not funny on a first date." Most of Jody's relationships have developed over time from friendships. Getting to know someone in a circle of friends takes the pressure off of making a good first impression. "I would prefer to meet someone in a more organic way," Jody says. "I don't perform that well."

addressing dating fears online

I type "dating seminar" into a search engine, hoping to find experts to address the dating challenges faced by George, Jody, and Emily, the challenges faced by all of us. I imagine I'll find a listing of a few gurus or companies that offer dating instruction. It turns out there are hundreds of results, and among the more promising is "Seven Essential Steps to Finding Love," a free two-hour seminar taught by Susan Page, author of books, including *If I'm So Wonderful, Why Am I Still Single?* I double-click, and my Real Player kicks in, offering me segments of the seminar. I can stop and start, much like a traffic-school course I took recently, except without the end-of-chapter quizzes.

I am unsure whether it is a sign of great progress or horrible descent into alienation that I can attend a seminar remotely in the privacy of my office or bedroom. It's hard to feel like I'm part of a group as I type alone on my computer with no one but a sleeping golden retriever to help fill the room. On the positive side, I have unlimited access to information at 9:00 P.M., now that I've finished my semi-pathetic dinner of baked potato with cottage cheese and Dijon mustard.

I already know we lead busy lives and that our work schedules make it harder than ever to meet someone we like enough to date. Now I am ready for Susan's explanation of just how we got this way. And what to do about it. Susan's seminar is a recorded version of the real thing, which was held in the San Francisco Bay Area sometime in the late '90s. But the Internet poses no such limitations on time or space. Susan asks her audience of two hundred men and women to tell her some of the reasons why they think they are still single. The responses are familiar relationship catchphrases: "Fear of rejection, inability to meet the right person, lack of time for dating, fear of commitment." Susan listens to some of the reasons, offers commentary on others. To the woman who says she's afraid she'll lose her independence and sense of self, Susan says, "We get set in our ways. It's hard to think of giving up our independence because we want intimacy." Susan considers all the reasons to be valid, even one that is clearly new to her: a man says he's single because he needs to marry a virgin or he won't be eligible to inherit a family estate.

Susan moves right on to her first theory about why men and women who say they want to be in relationships are still single. They fall into two categories: people who know what they are looking for but haven't found it, and people who say they want a relationship but are actually ambivalent.

Is that all there is to it?

choosing sides

Jody would consider herself someone who knows what she's looking for in a relationship, but she's coming up against roadblocks she never encountered before. At thirty-five, she's just hit the age that makes men she meets very nervous. "It is the sad by-product of dating in our thirties," says Jody. "Guys are thinking, 'Here I am, sitting across the table from a woman I would have to take seriously and marry if I were to date her, so I should never talk to her again.' If you're not a bimbo, guys think you have to be taken seriously." Attractive, athletic, and fair-haired, Jody has lived in cities around the country. But instead of viewing them as intriguing, men seem to think Jody's attributes are proof she wants to get married.

"When I meet guys they're assuming that I want it to continue. They have an overblown sense of their own power," Jody says. "They think that the future of the relationship is up to them because all I want is to keep dating them. They're thinking, 'Oh, I'm going to crush this woman.'

"Guys in their thirties are tripped out about feeling like they should be in a certain place in life," she goes on to say. "They think they should be married with kids even if they don't want to be. They think that they should be the provider, that they should have this good job. They do a whole weird number on themselves." Jody has hit the point where she sees the world in polar terms: if she wants to go out and have fun, she needs to date younger men. If she wants to be serious, she needs to find older men. Because men in their thirties have a difficult time figuring out how to behave around her. I wonder if these issues will come up in Susan's discussion.

virtual solutions

In her seminar, Susan holds forth on her two theories of why we're alone. Things look good for men and women who know what they want, Susan says, because eventually they will find it. They just have to keep dating and dating, exposing themselves to as many people as they can, until they find it. Susan cautions against believing we're too picky. "You just have to remember you haven't met the right person yet," she says. "If you believe you're going to succeed, you will. That is the key to finding love, as it is in every other area of life." And she leaves it at that.

But what of this first concept?

Just because we know what we want in a relationship, does it mean we want to spend our free time playing the odds until we stumble on the person who fits our criteria? Do we have a choice? I want to raise my hand. I want to ask Susan if searching for what we want, and not finding it, couldn't very well lead to a life of solitude. But there is no virtual hand to raise. Susan is out of range, and I can only go by the questions and answers that are available to me remotely.

Susan, like many other advice givers, refers to dating as a numbers game. But going on date after date can be mentally draining. Especially when the dates themselves are dismal. And dating is time-consuming. It could take months or even years to go out with the number of people required to find the needle in the haystack. Susan says that if there is a one in one hundred chance the next person you meet is a brilliant, romantic match, you may need to go out with ninety-nine other people before you find that one. Hence the popularity of speed-dating, in which twenty-five of those hundred can be knocked off in a single evening. "Your odds of finding love are exactly what you make them," Susan says. "Your odds have nothing to do with statistics. All you need is one person who is right. The smaller the odds, the more people you have to meet."

"I'm always going out, trying to meet people," Emily tells me. "Having a social life is just as much work as having a career.

There's no downtime." Even if Emily's not going out on dates, she's going out—partly because she just wants to keep busy and partly because there's always a chance she'll meet someone. "I have what I call the urban tribe factor—people my age who don't have anyone so we love each other. Mostly, it's just a group of people who hang out together and fill in each other's social lives because we're not on the couch with our boyfriends and girlfriends," she says.

And then there are the blind dates. Emily goes out with a smoker whose shoes and clothes reek so badly of cigarettes that she sends him home. "I thought I'd rather be home and in bed than on this date," Emily says. She goes out with a lawyer who takes her keys and drives her car to their dinner destination, flooring it while the car is in "park" and stripping the engine. Then Emily makes dinner plans with Keith, a thirty-four-year-old divorced banker who lives in a nice area, went to the right schools, and has the right jobs on his résumé. "My friend who set us up said that on paper we look like the perfect match," Emily says. Keith chooses an Italian place for dinner. Emily doesn't eat pasta but makes the best of it.

Emily talks about her plans to go to Burning Man, the annual festival in the Nevada desert. Conservative Keith feigns interest. The conversation turns to Keith's ex-wife, and Emily acts supportive. Drinks roll into dinner and Emily begins to think maybe it could work out, even though Keith is a little straitlaced for her taste. "So I invite him out to meet some friends at a dance club. I'll drive," she says. They hop into her car, a VW Bug, which has a bud vase built into the dashboard. "Then he makes some comment about how I go to Burning Man and have this hippie-dippie car with the flower in the bud vase," Emily says. She tells him her ex-boyfriend gave her the flower and she really likes it. Keith throws it out the window. "You don't need this anymore," he says.

Emily stops the car and goes out to pick up the flower. She puts it back in the vase, all the while wondering what kind of guy would do that. This time Keith takes the entire bud vase and chucks it over a wall so there's no way to find it. "So I'm just in shock," Emily says. "Why would he do that? Was he threatened because my ex-boyfriend gave it to me? Meanwhile we'd spent dinner talking about his ex-wife."

Emily and Keith get to the club where her friends are. Keith doesn't dance. Emily suggests he take a cab home. Another night, another date that goes nowhere. "There's always a trade-off. You go out with someone and you could be out with your friends or at the gym. So if you don't like the guy, you just feel like 'Why am I here?'" she says.

Across town, George agrees to go with a friend to a singles event in which everyone wears a name tag with one-half of a pickup line. "Mine said, 'Is your father a farmer?' I don't even know what that means. It doesn't sound like a pickup line." But the worst was still to come. George and his friend enter a large room at an event venue called Broadway Studios and find a bucket of pencils and paper accompanying a sign that says, DON'T LEAVE WITHOUT DIGITS.

"It was so depressing," George says. "I'd have what I thought was a good conversation with an attractive girl and get her number and then I'd see her a half hour later across the room, talking to someone else and giving her number to another guy."

Jody, too, plays the numbers to no avail. "For smart, professional women who have done a lot, the hurdle rate for someone new is high," says Jody. "Last year I dated three guys. The first one I was crazy about but he was crazy. He's flaky, can't make a plan. I'm too busy for someone who can't make a plan. The second was perfect on paper, had a PhD, had his own business, he's in a band. But he's not a good communicator. He's inexperienced in relationships, and I felt like I can't school this guy." The third is a guy Jody went to college with, who wanted to turn their relationship into a romantic one. "The underlying problem was that I wasn't attracted to him and it's not like I needed the guy to be universally gorgeous, just attractive to me. I'm not willing to give up on that front," Jody says.

"I'm already looking at a future relationship and thinking, 'What am I going to have to give up in terms of things that are important to me?'" Jody says. "I want to meet someone who likes the outdoors, who is smart, attractive. I am like that, so why can't I find someone who is like that as well? In economics they call it a matching problem."

no one wants to settle

Women's ambivalence about settling for an imperfect relationship is not a new concept. In the late eighteenth and early nineteenth centuries, young women had new opportunities to attend school and get jobs. But their growing independence made some women much more ambivalent about marriage, which threatened to squelch their newfound freedoms. The number of unmarried women reached an unprecedented 11 percent by the early nineteenth century, according to the University of Houston Web site, Digital History.

Age at first marriage was higher in 1890 than in the decades since—26.1 for men and 22 for women, according to the U.S. Census Bureau. Through most of the twentieth century, many men and women married younger, right out of high school or college, when they had the greatest exposure to the dating pool. It wasn't until the 1980s that the median age at first marriage rose to 1890s levels. And now we're waiting longer, on average. The median age at first marriage in 2002 was 25.3 for women, compared to 26.9 for men, according to the Census Bureau. Marrying later allows us to establish ourselves in careers and gain a sense of our independent selves. But it distances us from the pool of dates we had in college. Now we're left with the dilemma of how to find each other or, according to Susan, whether we even want to.

susan tackles ambivalence

The focus of Susan's seminar is the second category of reasons why we are single, all of which stem from some form or another of inner ambivalence about whether we actually want to be in a relationship. It would seem on its surface fairly obvious to each of us whether we want to be coupled or whether we prefer being single. Susan says we need to look beneath the surface. She asks each person in the group to imagine he or she is going to meet the perfect romantic partner the following day. This would be the person who meets all our expectations of what we want in a relationship. "Now take out an index card and write down all the ways your life would change for the better, all the things you'd gain for meeting this person." She gives us ninety seconds to make a list. "Now turn over the card and make a list of all the things you'd lose if you were in a relationship with your ideal partner."

Susan asks the group to pair up, men with women, and to discuss the lists. There are a few moments of incomprehensible mumbling coming through the speakers on my computer. Then everyone is encouraged to share what they learned from the exercise. I am at a loss since there are no men in my home office who will compare notes with me. I turn up the volume and listen to Susan's group.

"I thought I had no ambivalence but then I came up with a long list of what I would lose," one woman says.

"I realized there are some of us who are a lot more ready for relationships than others," says one of the men in the group.

Another man says that his partner in the exercise listed the long discussions that come with relationships as a downside. "But I realized I'm looking forward to them, to the tough parts." The women in the seminar clamor for his phone number.

"I initially put that I'd lose my freedom if I was in a relationship, but then I realized that if I was really with the perfect partner, he'd let me have the freedom I need," says another woman. The responses continue along those lines.

"You need to ask for one hundred percent of what you want one hundred percent of the time," concludes Susan. "If both parties agree to do that, the relationship will work."

Susan's seminar seems to get to the heart of what people want to know. It helps them expose some of the things they may not have been aware of without being preachy or filled with psychological double-talk. In Susan's opinion, many of us are single because we already have a lot of things we're afraid of losing in a relationship. We like our autonomy. We like to be able to keep whatever we want in the refrigerator and to come and go as we please. She describes us as single wolves in relationship clothing. In other words, we relate to people who are married or in relationships; we consider ourselves the types that will one day be in relationships, but we don't actually have to put up with any of the negative aspects of being in relationships. We can have all the fun that single people have without associating ourselves with the stereotype of perpetually single adults. But she encourages us to realize that just because we're happy being single, it doesn't mean we aren't interested in love. "You can live fully as a single person and be clear that your goal is to be in a relationship," she says.

Susan's solution is to behave as though we are not ambivalent, to act as if love is the highest priority in life. She says most of us shy away from relationships out of fear: fear of commitment, fear of abandonment, fear of rejection. "Ask yourselves," she instructs, "will you let your fear stop you from getting what you want? You need to experience your fears, put them into the trunk, and climb into the driver's seat." She even points to an odd role model, Babe Ruth: when he was in front of a hostile crowd, she says, he pointed his bat toward center field and hit the ball directly there.

It is something to think about.

in san francisco

The more I get to know Emily and George, the more I start to wonder if they might be a good match. Both say they are willing to be set up on a blind date, so I put them in touch via e-mail. George has been on three dates with a woman he met at a party and can tell it's not going anywhere, so he sends Emily an e-mail. She responds promptly and says she's very interested but that she's pretty busy for the next few weeks. George waits and e-mails her again, wondering if her schedule has freed up. Emily says she's still busy. "I don't have time to chase someone down who I don't even know," George says. He doesn't e-mail her again. For her part, Emily says she just doesn't have the energy to go out on another blind date. "I have my urban tribe. We're a close-knit, self-sufficient group, so it's a comfortable fallback and another reason not to go out with new people," she says.

But Emily does not consider herself ambivalent about wanting a relationship. Almost to prove the point, she decides to move out of a great apartment in a nice part of town that is the envy of anyone looking for a place to live in San Francisco. She's going to live with two friends instead. "I'm scared of getting used to being alone. I'm worried that I'm setting myself up for spinsterhood," Emily says. "If I'm around people, I'm more likely to meet people. And I'll be more used to compromising and sharing my space, which I'll need to be in a relationship."

Jody has been through that line of reasoning and talked herself down. "There's a pervasive feeling that a night spent home watching TV is a squandered opportunity to find someone to date," Jody says. "A year and a half ago, I used to always try to have something to do." She was concerned that she needed to be out where there was potential to meet men. But there was a larger issue at the heart of it: the fear that one Saturday night at home would be a sign of things to come. "I try to squelch the inclination to think that if I'm home on a Saturday night, it is the start of a trajectory at the end of which I will die alone," Jody says. All the same, Jody does make an effort to go out, even when she doesn't feel like it. "It is helpful to overcome some inertia. Like that adage that eighty percent of life is showing up," she says. "I like to go to things just so I can say, 'Okay, I did it. Now I know I'm not missing anything.'"

remote messages

As far as I can tell, the two hundred participants in San Francisco seem satisfied with Susan's information. But I stop and consider what I, or anyone else who is taking this seminar remotely, might be missing. The technology we have at our fingertips teaching us how to meet each other is preventing us from doing just that. Part of the benefit of attending Susan's seminar in person is that there are one hundred men and one hundred women, all single, all presumably in the room because they want to find a good person to date. A side benefit of listening to Susan talk may very well be a conversation with a stranger who might make a good future date.

Susan ends her seminar by discussing the seven things we all have to do to succeed at finding love. She talks about acting as though we believe we'll succeed and about giving up on the idea that finding a mate will be fun. On the contrary, it takes work, Susan says. She tells us to form a master plan for how we'll meet the person of our dreams. "The right method to meet the person of your dreams is the last method you will use," she says, encouraging us to fill our calendars with mate-meeting activities. She emphasizes the statistical aspects of love, telling us to go for volume and avoid limiting ourselves to those we think of as our type.

As a point in case, Susan talks about how she met her own husband at a friend's house. She wanted a man who was tall, handsome, and successful and she met a man who was short and bald and worked as a ceramic artist. Susan's impression was that he was a "hippie potter who dropped out and couldn't get his life together so he sells mugs on Telegraph Avenue." By the fourth date, Susan knew they'd probably get married. Six months later, they did. She concludes: "If I just went for the type I wanted, look at what I would have missed." Though a charming story, it calls into question Susan's first assumption about knowing what we want and eventually finding it. Maybe we need to be open to what we think we don't want.

But in the end, how is that different from settling? From my desktop, it's impossible for me to ask.

Animals frequently toss their heads in order to solicit attention. Courting women do it regularly; they raise their shoulders, arch their backs, and toss their locks in a single sweeping motion. Albatross toss their heads and snap their bills between bouts of nodding, bowing and rubbing bills together.

FROM *Anatomy of Love: A Natural History of Mating, Marriage, and Why We Stray,* BY HELEN FISHER, 1992

10.

a flirting lesson for
the plumage-challenged

The room fills slowly. The room always seems to fill slowly, even when there's a designated time for an event to begin. People amble in and assort themselves in a random scatter pattern, one person per row, none actually sitting close enough for immediate contact. Ironic, really, since we are all here to improve our interpersonal skills. But if we were a room full of people capable of launching into comfortable banter with one another, we probably wouldn't be paying $45 apiece to attend a flirting seminar on a Sunday night. The seminar is held at a hotel in the hip River North area of Chicago. It conjures up an image of a swanky scene. The actual location, however, conjures up a boring corporate team-building event.

It's hard to avoid sizing people up. I notice one exceptionally tall man across the aisle from me, sitting up in his chair, looking straight ahead like a tree in a petrified forest. A couple of rows in front of me is a balding man who is busy poring over notes that turn out to be from a prior course he took on flirting. And there is a woman, a few rows ahead of the tall guy, who shifts uncomfortably in her chair, crossing and uncrossing her legs under a flowered dress. It is like the first day at a new school. A lot of nervous smiles and furtive glances as we wait for the teacher to give us some direction.

fashionably late flirtation

Carrie is late. Carrie is our self-proclaimed love guru, who will guide us through the treacherous waters of flirting techniques and teach us to survive without getting eaten alive. I wonder if being late is part of her technique. Maybe it's flirting by fire. She figures if she leaves two dozen socially inept people in a room together, maybe we will be forced to begin flirting out of sheer boredom.

Ten minutes in, boredom seems to be winning. Then Linda, a vivacious, dark-haired woman in a red-and-black wraparound skirt, walks to the front of the room. "I'm not Carrie, but I do know her. She is a friend of mine," she says. "And I just want to tell you that you are in for a special evening. Carrie just has a way about her, and she has such valuable insight into how men and women relate."

It's a tough crowd. No one is matching Linda's cheery vibe.

For a moment, I feel sorry for Carrie, about to enter a room full of people who won't crack a smile. But this is Carrie's business. I imagine she is used to it by now. I should feel sorrier for Linda, trying to kill time while we grow ever more restless.

By the time Carrie arrives, the room has gotten more crowded. There are twenty of us—eleven women, nine men. No one looks much younger than midthirties except for one broad-shouldered, towheaded guy who walks in with an older brunette woman who turns out to be his mother.

Carrie fills the room, right down to the practiced tinkle of her laugh. She wears magenta lipstick and smiles broadly while she speaks, showing off a prominent set of possibly-oversized teeth. Her wavy hair is a highlighted sandy brown and hangs down her back. She uses it to demonstrate flirtatious behavior, softly shifting it over her shoulders, past gold dangling earrings, or brushing it out of her eyes. Carrie is the adult, large-boned version of a giggly schoolgirl, tottering around the room in a pair of low spike-heeled pumps. She wears a navy blue, embroidered, long-sleeved blouse, buttoned tightly over her bust, and flowing, sheer black, wide-legged skirt-pants, which have an actual pair of filmy pants under what looks like a skirt slit to the waistband. It's basic urban camouflage, which makes it just hard enough to tell what's going on with the skirt-and-pants combination that it distracts the brain from noticing any figure flaws. Unless someone stands in front of you for three hours, wearing black sheer skirt-pants.

disco balls in her eyes

It is easy to see why Carrie is good at talking to people. She is confident but not intimidating. Plainly put, she is not someone who women would find threatening, yet she's someone who men would still feel flattered by if she took an interest in them. "The key to flirting is that you have to have a party in your head," Carrie says, launching right into the course. "I have a party in my head all the time." Carrie smiles, waiting for the information to register. We look at her blankly. She continues, undeterred. "And when you go out, you have to bring the party with you."

This is all well and fine in theory, but in practice most of us are tired at the end of a long day. If we're going anywhere, it's to find the party someplace else, not to provide it. If I had a party in my head all the time, it would definitely limit the kinds of activities I'd pursue. But I am not Carrie. With her party and her skirt-pants, she would have no trouble flirting with a floor lamp or a potted plant.

Carrie speaks loudly, as if to infuse the group with excitement about the wonders of flirting. "I am going to tell you about the most important flirting technique: the triple drive-by rule."

It's a variant on the old professorial tool which says that students will remember information if it is presented to them three times. Carrie recommends finding someone to flirt with and approaching that person three times within an hour to make a big impression. "Most women just buzz the tower," Carrie says, using terminology reminiscent of the movie *Top Gun* to criticize the way women make a minimal effort to let a man know he is being flirted with. If the man does not pick up on the subtle effort, the party is over.

Men, for their part, do not help the situation. "Guys are in such disbelief that a woman is actually talking to them that they don't realize she's flirting. So the women eventually give up," says Carrie. The triple drive-by rule necessitates multiple, carefully planned visits to the object of one's flirting affections—first to lay the groundwork, then to drive the point home, and lastly, to leave an impression.

Men are instructed to begin with a subtle comment. "Think of it as a drop of water landing in the desert," she says. The next time he approaches, a man is supposed to give the woman more time to check him out. Finally, he goes in for a final swoop, and the woman is hooked. "That's when she'll be likelier to have a longer conversation."

People begin taking notes. Maybe it's just a knee-jerk reaction to being in a classroom setting. Or maybe we feel like these are valuable lessons we're likely to forget when we leave the room. Carrie looks around with her bright pink lipstick smile as though she's leading us to the promised land.

I begin to wonder how we've drifted so far from our ability to talk to one another. Pheasants who wail out mating calls are not stymied by overthinking. They preen their feathers and answer each other's plaintive cries because that's what you do when you're a pheasant. And it works. Ducks preen and flirt, ducks mate, and ducklings are born shortly thereafter. A far cry from our animal descendants, we seem to have lost our innate ability to flirt and have to rely on a studied approach to basic human relationships. Or does it just seem that way?

breathless encounters

"Now, everyone let out a big sigh," Carrie instructs. Twenty people inhale and let out a low groan. "Now, just the men," she says. The groan gets lower and deeper. "Now, just the women." The sigh takes on a high-pitched, breathier quality.

"Now, isn't that sexy?" Carrie wants to know. The sighing is part of a flirting technique designed to relax the vocal chords, allowing flirters to speak to their targets in a more relaxed way. "It's subliminal, sexy," Carrie says. "Let someone hear your personality without words."

The sighing is supposed to act as a subtle signal to our autonomic nervous systems to chill out. According to Carrie, flirting begins with spotting someone across the crowded room and letting out a big sigh to relax ourselves and our voices. Then we need to "send that person a subconscious smile" before we walk up and try our three-tiered approach to insinuating ourselves into a conversation.

All I know is that all the thinking, preparing, and sighing make an actual conversation feel like a loaded gun.

trying the techniques

Our next assignment is to practice sighing and easing into flirty conversation with one another. "Sigh and say, 'Wow, what a work schedule I've had. I could sure use some time at a spa.' Go on, say that to each other," Carrie says.

We each turn to a neighbor and repeat her words. "Now, practice saying this: 'What relaxes you more—visiting a new place or an old, familiar standby?'" We obey. Little, forged conversations ensue.

"So, where would you go?" my assigned flirting neighbor asks me. I immediately panic. Somehow my brain can't make the leap from prescribed question-and-answer material to actual conversation. It is like memorizing a bunch of facts for a test and then freezing because the question isn't phrased exactly the way it appeared on the study sheet. Carrie didn't tell us where to say we'd like to go on vacation. And I can't jump-start myself back into the way I would normally communicate with people every day. Suddenly, I'm a pheasant who's too tongue-tied to yelp out a return mating call to my feathered friend.

Carrie admits that it's a problem that we do not have the same kinds of flirting mechanisms available to other invertebrates. When a duck wants to mate, he dunks his head underwater a few times and looks around to see if any females in the area follow suit, Carrie tells us. If that goes well, the duck sings a little song, which interested females will mimic. When the male has identified the female who is most interested in his behavior, the mating begins. We have stifled our own innate mating signals, according to Carrie, so we need to embellish on what we've got.

in theory

Carrie proposes a way to drum up interest in ourselves. It is part of her theory that we can "change our reality at will," just by behaving differently.

She tells all the men to form a line at the front of the room, facing all the women. We are told to stand up in front of our chairs. "Now, ladies, twirl around in a circle in front of your chairs and say, 'I'm irresistible.'" We look at each other. Is she serious? If twirling and rolling our eyes at the same time is a sign of physical dexterity, we all score well. The move is supposed to be another way to relax us into the proper mind-set for flirting. After sighing to relax our vocal chords, we are supposed to twirl in front of men and tell them how irresistible we are. Because we don't have colorful feathers and birdsongs, we'll just do the next best thing.

"Now, guys, didn't they look sexy?" There is a general mumble of approval from our male counterparts. "And, ladies, didn't that make you feel sexier?" Again, a mutter that was taken as a sign of agreement.

Do I feel sexy? Absolutely not. I feel silly. I feel self-conscious. But there is nothing about twirling in front of ten men I don't know that makes me feel more confident about talking to strangers. If anything, I am reliving my first day in high-school drama class when I was told to walk across the stage in the manner of someone sad. The exercise reduces any poise and confidence I have to practically zero.

Even though these are men who are taking a class on flirting, indicating that they're open to new ideas, I still care whether they think we look like idiots. And I kind of have the feeling we do.

Then it is their turn. "Now, guys, get down on one knee," Carrie instructs. I wonder if part of proper flirting includes proposing to a woman as a way of getting her attention. I wouldn't put it past Carrie. "Now, say, 'I really want a relationship.'" The men obey. "Now, say, 'I really, really want a relationship. Please, let me have a relationship.'" Again, they obey. I realize the one being proposed to must be some sort of higher power that is supposed to deliver on the promise. "Now, let out a big wolf whistle and say, 'Ooh, baby.'" Ten men let out their inner construction worker and grin as they say the words that are off-limits to any man a woman doesn't know very well.

This seems to be their favorite part. We are supposed to find it flattering. Or maybe it is just some kind of payoff for them for stepping up to the plate and admitting they want a, gasp, relationship.

"Ladies, didn't you find them attractive when they said they wanted a relationship?" The women seem to agree.

preening our feathers

Carrie tells the men to sit on one side of the room, and the women on the other, turning our chairs to face off. "Now, ladies, don't just sit back in your chairs. Sit on the edge of your seats, arch your backs, and smile," she says. We perch uneasily on the edges of our chairs, which inadvertently forces us to arch our backs to keep from falling off. "Now, you can pivot and look around the room."

I am reminded of ladies in knee-high, lace-up boots, festooned skirts, and big colored feathers on their hats. No one else perches on a chair like this.

"When you sit like this, you look interested," Carrie tells us. She asks the men to give their opinions. They nod in general agreement that we look interested. Or just interesting. "Don't be afraid to take up space," Carrie says. "Don't close off your body."

I perch on the edge of my chair and almost fall forward, taking the chair with me. Carrie, ever the toothy optimist, would probably just chalk it up to an excellent icebreaker. I sneak a look at the men watching us. Some of them are visibly suppressing laughter.

Carrie wants some feedback. "How do you feel, ladies? Do you feel sexy?" She calls on Jean, the woman to my left. "Sure. I feel like I look a little more available," Jean says.

Next, Carrie points to me. "How about you? How do you feel?" I am honest. I tell her that I feel uncomfortable, that I doubt I could sit like this for very long, even with hours of yoga training as practice. "I feel like I could flirt more easily if I were comfortable," I say. "And I'd be more comfortable sitting back in my chair." Carrie waves a hand in front of me as if to make me disappear. I am not helping her sell her point.

Then the men get a turn for some playacting. They are told to stand up in front of their chairs and to close their eyes. "Now, say to yourselves, 'Women find me attractive.' Then picture yourselves with a woman who really likes you," Carrie says. Most, if not all, of the men smile. And some of them puff their chests out and stand up a little taller.

"Now, imagine that no one likes you," Carrie says. The men put on sad faces. One of them visibly deflates. She tells them to open their eyes and give her feedback on how it felt to imagine themselves as attractive creatures that women find appealing.

"I felt good. I felt like I stood up a little taller," says Ted, an ad salesman.

"Exactly!" Carrie says. "And, ladies, didn't you find them much more attractive when they had a positive image in their heads?" We mumble in agreement. These gestures are actually rooted in animal behavior. According to anthropologist Helen Fisher, author of *Why We Love*, standing tall is a basic posture, common to codfish and mule deer alike. Swelling, puffing up, and even chest pounding are all meant to signal dominance and prowess. Carrie is merely putting us in touch with our inner gorilla.

in practice

Next, Carrie asks Todd and Alice to come to the front of the room for a participatory demonstration. Alice stands in front of Todd, with her hands clasped in her lap. "No fig leaves," teases Carrie. "Men like to stuff their hands into their pockets and jiggle something, and women like to cover themselves up in some way," Carrie says. "The best flirting position is with your hands dropped down at your sides."

Suddenly my arms seem to be eight feet long. It is very difficult to feel comfortable with dangling arms. Arms feel like they need to be doing something—holding a drink, keeping close tabs on a purse, keeping our pants from falling down.

"Now, Todd, give Alice a compliment. Whatever comes to mind," Carrie says.

"That's a nice color you're wearing," Todd says, clearly embarrassed to be saying it in front of a room full of people. Alice is wearing a royal blue brocaded jacket that looks like a kimono.

"Ooh, but you used a four-letter word. Never say the word 'nice' to a woman," Carrie says. "Try it again."

"That's an interesting color you're wearing," Todd says.

"Ooh, interesting. The kiss of death. No one wants to be told they look interesting. It's hard to know if that's good or bad," Carrie says.

"Okay, that is a vibrant shade of blue. I really like it," Todd says out of desperation.

"Thank you," Alice says.

"Great. That is successful flirting," Carrie tells them, allowing them to return to their seats. Todd is red-faced, and Alice looks like she's sweating beneath her nice, interesting, vibrant blue jacket.

Apparently, successful flirting can also masquerade as a ballsy come-on. "Ladies, if you meet a man in a bar and he's wearing a tie, just grab his tie and say, 'This tie is fabulous. Can I borrow it when you're done with it?'" Forget the implication of lewd behavior. I wonder if Carrie believes we are totally incapable of normal human interaction. It seems like an invasion to start grabbing people's clothing.

Carrie disagrees. She says that the good thing about fondling a man's clothing is that it puts a woman in his personal space and sends a direct signal that she is flirting. Carrie's theory is that often men are not sure whether a woman is actually flirting with them or whether she's just being friendly. So, many of her meeting ploys are simply ways of letting a man know that this is no accidental encounter.

Apparently, some men are more thickheaded than others. For the truly dense, Carrie has a ready-made solution: a T-shirt that says "I'm a flirt." For those of us unwilling to wear our intentions on our chests, there is the flirting hat. Again, these are ways to get attention, to subtly break the ice. For all our subtlety, we might as well just carry signs around, announcing that we are flirting.

It turns out that is an option we'll hear about later.

mixing, mingling, and stuffing the coffers

We are given a ten-minute break. It turns out that flirting is too complicated to learn about in one sitting. During the break, Carrie assigns us the task of shaking the hands of at least three people while we stretch our legs and meander into the hotel hallway.

I introduce myself to the woman sitting next to me and shake her hand. "Hi, I'm Stacy," I say. "Do you think this counts as one of my three people?"

"I don't know," she says. "I'm Mary."

I take my assignment seriously. I decide to shake the hand of the guy sitting one row ahead of me, the one to whom I had to bemoan my day and discuss vacation plans earlier. Now, it feels much more comfortable, like a normal conversation, rather than a follow-up to a practiced flirting ploy.

Our vacation discussion had led to talk of Paris. "When was the last time you were in Paris?" I ask.

"Oh, it's probably been ten years," he says. "But I'd love to go back."

"You should. I'm Stacy," I say, extending my hand. Make no mistake, I am not achieving successful flirting action. I am barely hanging on to his attention. But he probably realizes I'm going to be sitting behind him for the remainder of the course, so he humors me and shakes my hand. "Pete. Nice to meet you. So why are you here?"

I tell him I've always been interested in what a person could learn at a seminar like this one, so I finally decided to try it out. "How about you?" I ask Pete.

"Oh, I could definitely use some help in the flirting department. Whenever I talk to women, I always end up as friends. Somehow I'm not able to convey anything romantic."

"Hmm, I have different issues when I meet people. I tend to be on the shy side, so people tend to think I'm closed off because I'm not friendly right away," I tell him.

"You seem friendly to me," Pete tells me.

"Thanks," I say, suddenly realizing the primary problem with this entire course. Carrie never addresses our own individual socializing issues. In a room with only twenty people, it would be easy to open up a comfortable discussion. That way, she'd be able to address the reasons why each of us ended up here. But her impression must have been that her generalized advice and techniques would be a "one size fits all" for any issues the group might have.

Pete and I refill our water glasses and walk back into the room. Carrie has set up a display of books she has written on flirting techniques, and pamphlets with information about three-day flirting and relationship retreats she holds in San Antonio, Texas. Carrie also has folders of important flirting handouts that are presented as "course materials" to be purchased for $10 and necessary for the second half of the class. Each folder has a pink, heart-shaped Post-it on the front.

When the cash box comes out, it becomes clear that, all concern about our romantic futures aside, this evening is about commerce. Carrie, a former travel agent, has built an entire business around selling advice to people who are worried they have flirting barriers. She is not unlike any other businessperson who has figured out a way to grow an empire, based on other people's fears and insecurities.

The flirty, giggly side of Carrie is subsumed by the businesswoman. She becomes ultraorganized, collecting cash and checks in exchange for folders of flirting pamphlets. Her pink smile disappears. Her fingers fly over the buttons of an adding machine. The stack of folders dwindles. We sit with our goods, a few daring to open the folders and peek at what lies ahead. I scan through the contents, much of which are a recap of the pickup lines we've been taught, intermixed with invitations to purchase Carrie's newsletters and books and forms to register for more seminars and retreats.

waving at no one

The break is over. We retake our places in the room and look up at Carrie like hungry little pups, waiting for the next morsel of advice to be doled out. Carrie admits that it can be difficult to arrive at a party or walk into a bar alone. Even with a party in your head. But the key, she says, is to convey the impression that you're comfortable, that you're someone others would want to get to know. "Walk in and look across the room, then smile and wave like you recognize a good friend," Carrie says. By smiling, we will look approachable and friendly. She recalls a time when she went to a bar alone and thought to herself that she could never actually wave across the room. This was back in the days when she was shy, she recalls. But she found herself waving. At no one.

"I just smiled and waved as though I belonged there," she says. "And you know what? I looked friendly, like someone you'd like to get to know better. I met more men that night than I ever did before."

According to Carrie, the difficulty in meeting and flirting stems from walls that we put up toward the outside world. "Each of us has five barriers to flirting," she says. Not everyone has the same five barriers, but we all have them, she says: "They include fear of rejection, shyness, difficulty in new situations, fear of commitment, you name it." In other words, each of us has hang-ups that prevent us from embracing the idea of talking to a stranger. This is not news. But getting past these barriers is not simply a question of having Carrie give us a cute opening line. For a shy person, it's difficult to start talking to a stranger, and no three-hour seminar is going to erase that completely.

Practicing sighing and getting comfortable saying one-liners is a surface solution to a bigger problem: we have all experienced rejection and are reluctant to put ourselves out there for another drubbing. The older we get, the more lessons we've learned, and unfortunately many of them are negative messages that make us gun-shy the next time around. Instead of walking through life with a party in our heads, most of us are just trying to get through the day without having our egos bashed. It's a long road between the two. Carrie has her work cut out for her.

playing the fool

"Take a name-tag sticker and write your name on it, then stick it on your back upside-down. People will feel bad for you and start talking to you to let you know it's there," Carrie suggests. Part of flirting is simply getting up the nerve to talk to someone, even if that means tricking people into talking to you first.

She points to the red-and-black folders that hold our flirting handouts and instructs us to peel off the pink heart-shaped sticker on the cover. "These are just heart-shaped Post-it notes from Staples," she says. "I suggest you go out and buy a whole package of them and carry them with you to use as props."

She really means it. Carrie suggests that a great way to break the ice with a stranger is to present the heart-shaped sticker and ask, "If I give you my heart, will you promise to take care of it?"

The first problem is that I can come up with about ten not-very-nice things I'd probably be thinking if someone came up to me and presented me with a heart-shaped sticker. And if there was alcohol involved, there's a good chance I might actually say some of them.

I look around the room. There are a few people who are smiling, apparently pleased to have learned a new pickup line. Others roll their eyes like they would not be caught dead taunting a stranger with a paper heart.

The hearts are not the only props Carrie suggests we use. She hands each of us two rolled pieces of parchment which look rather official. One of them is our "flirter's diploma." I assume this is the parting gift we get for finishing a flirting seminar. I picture Carrie sending us off into the world like little sparrows leaving the nest with our flirting diplomas. "Go forth and flirt," I imagine she'll say.

The flirting diploma has no such opaque purpose. It is, in fact, meant to be used in public places where flirting is a possibility. Carrie suggests handing it to the object of admiration and saying, "I took this class and they gave me a flirting permit. Do I have your permission to flirt with you?" The idea is that the other person will ask to see the diploma, and a conversation free of awkwardness will ensue.

I secretly believe that Carrie thinks the cards are a way to drum up more business. "Oh, you took a class to learn how to flirt? And you're so good at it. Maybe I should take that course, too."

Carrie also hands each of us a little conversation-starting cheat sheet in the form of a second piece of rolled-up paper. This one features the key flirting phrase, "Is there someone in your life who would mind if I asked you to dance?" The card specifies that we have the option of substituting words for "dance," as appropriate. But the purpose of all the props is singular: to state explicitly that we are flirting.

Joan, a woman in her forties who's been quiet until now, raises her hand. "So these are just pickup lines, right?" A hush falls over the room. Is Carrie going to be offended by the inference that her carefully honed techniques are mere pickup lines?

"I don't like to think of it that way," Carrie says, looking at the ceiling as if summoning her inner calm. "These are techniques, ways of breaking the ice with someone so the flirting can begin."

Joan takes a slurp of her drink and nods. It's not clear whether she's buying Carrie's rationale or just giving up the fight.

John brings the discussion down to statistics. "When advertisers send out fliers to the general public, asking them to try a new soft drink, they know most people are going to throw them away. But if just one-tenth of one percent tries the soft drink, they've more than made their money back. It's the same with dating."

the rules of active flirtation

Carrie divides us into groups of four. "Now, I'm going to teach you some active-flirtation techniques," she says. "The trick is to practice flirting by yourself so you'll be relaxed in front of someone else. Get all your nervous, hurried flirting done on your own first."

My foursome includes a tall, sweet-looking man with an accent, a woman with a pixie hairdo, and the young towheaded guy who came with his mom. We stand up and face one another. "Now," says Carrie, "turn to someone in your group and say, 'Hi, my name is so-and-so, what's your name?' Say it two times fast and one time slow."

The idea, Carrie says, is to get used to saying the mouthful of words at high speed so that when we say them at a more relaxed pace, we ourselves are more relaxed.

The blond guy, whose name is Chris, grabs my hand, as though to shake it. I get through "Hi, my name is" when he chimes in with "Hi, my name is Chris; Hi, my name is Chris"; then slowly, "Hi. My . . . name . . . is . . . Chris."

"How was that?" he asks.

"It was fine," I tell him. "But I don't think we're supposed to say it at the same time."

"Okay, let's try again." Chris still has a death grip on my hand. "Hi, my name is Chris; Hi, my name is Chris." He pauses and slows his pace to a halting degree. "Hi. My . . . name . . . is . . . Chris." He wipes some sweat from his brow. "Would you date me if I came up to you in a bar and said that?"

"I might think it was strange that you were introducing yourself to me three times. But otherwise, sure, why not?" I tell him.

We summon Carrie over to find out. "You're supposed to get used to saying it fast when you're on your own, so when you meet someone you want to flirt with, you're used to saying it and you can sound relaxed."

I take my turn. "Hi, my name is Stacy. What's your name? Hi, my name is Stacy. What's your name?" I say at top speed, then normally: "Hi. My name is Stacy. What's your name?"

"Okay," Chris says. "The third time you definitely sounded more relaxed."

Once we're finished with our introductions, we are supposed to switch to another partner within our foursome and try it again. But the other two in our foursome are still practicing their techniques on each other. Chris and I talk about what brought him to a flirting seminar. "I figure it's always good to have things to say to girls when I go out with my friends," Chris says, adding that his mother has gone to several of Carrie's courses and encouraged him to attend.

Our next assignment is to introduce ourselves again. Only this time, we are supposed to use a strange voice. Carrie demonstrates in an uncomfortably high octave. "Hi, my name is Carrie. What's your name?" she says, sounding like a little canary.

Chris and I look at each other. I am wracking my brain, trying to figure out if I am even capable of a different voice. Chris goes first. "Hi, my name is Chris. Hi, my name is Chris," he says quickly in a slightly deeper voice, which is imperceptibly different from his normal voice. Then, one time slowly: "Hi, my name is Chris. Okay, which did you like the best? I tried three different voices."

I don't have the heart to tell him that to my ears, all three voices sounded the same. "The last one. That was the best."

"Yeah, I felt like that one was good," he says.

Now it's my turn. I go through the "hi, my name is" exercise using some version of a southern accent, feeling all the while like a poor proxy for Dolly Parton.

"That was good. I liked that accent. Where was that from?" Chris asks.

"I'm not really sure. Either Texas or somewhere like Virginia," I say, figuring I am in the ballpark.

Our active-flirtation lesson is far from over. One of Carrie's surefire ploys is to call out to a man across the room, "Excuse me, I just have to tell you you're really cute." She suggests doing this whenever we see someone we want to meet. "There isn't a guy in the world who wouldn't appreciate hearing that from a woman." This is one instance when it's okay to break the four-letter-word rule, Carrie says. Using four-letter descriptions for men is just fine, she says. Yet she doesn't bother to ask the ten men in the room what they think about it. Which seems odd.

All night I've been trying to figure out what we're learning.

It's not at all clear what the fake accents have to do with flirting, except to make us comfortable trying different versions of ourselves. But if a person is not comfortable walking up to a complete stranger and starting a conversation, how is a fake accent going to pave the way to feeling at ease?

When it comes down to it, we are all just trying to meet one another, whether that comes under the guise of needing better flirting techniques or wanting easier modes of introduction. We want to know where to find one another and know what to say when we get there. And it should be innate. But we've made it difficult, so much so that we can't find one another at all without help. And we'll believe almost anyone who tells us what to say because it must surely be better than what we've dreamed up on our own. But is it better just because we've paid for it? Or is it just profitable for the ones who've chosen to capitalize on our struggle?

a wingman by any other name is still a wingman

Carrie calls Mike and Jeremy to the front of the room. "Mike, you walk to the back of the room, and, Jeremy, you follow a few feet behind him like you don't know him." They obey. The rest of us watch them.

"When you're in a bar, you should always pair up with a friend," says Carrie. "One of you can walk ahead, and the other one can watch to see what women are checking him out." She is serious. Carrie imparts this advice with cheekiness, as though the men in the room are hearing gospel that they couldn't possibly dream up on their own. Most men I interviewed are already familiar with the concept. Some call it "taking a lap."

And Carrie has another tidbit. The next time they are at the supermarket, she suggests that the men in the room go to the meat section, hold up a rump roast, and say loudly, "How do you fry this thing?" She guarantees that a few single women will come to the rescue.

The supermarket can be an equal-opportunity flirting venue, Carrie tells us. There is no better chance to find topics of conversation than in a place that is filled with props. We are set free to ask our fellow shoppers what they think of the spaghetti sauce they are buying. And if we are really sly, we will be able to ascertain whether that desirable shopper in the lane next to ours is buying a Lean Cuisine for one or shopping for a family. "Look in the basket of a guy you want to meet and ask about what he's eating for dinner," she says. Sure. And why not ask if he wants help downing that big fried rump roast?

Carrie has answers for everything. She anticipates that we might not feel like we're the right type of people to flirt well, that we're not good at it. But, she says, we can adopt flirting like adopting a different personality for just one evening. "Try flirting on like a coat when it's cold outside. Just try it on when you go out," she says.

It's not that this wouldn't be good advice, if we do, in fact, feel that we aren't the natural types to try flirting. And perhaps some of us do feel that way. But Carrie never asks. She assumes that the reason we can't flirt, that the reason we're attending her course, is that we don't feel like we're the flirting types. And by assuming that, she misses out on really knowing what we're all thinking. She neglects to find out what our real barriers are. Her advice is of the "one size fits all" variety. And muumuus don't look good on anybody.

All this flirting is just a process of gathering potential dates, says Carrie. The object is to have options when it comes to our social lives. It's silly to focus on one or two people when it comes to flirting and dating. "You want to think of yourself as having a basket. And then you want to keep as many potential dates as you can in that basket," she says. Keeping all your eggs in one basket doesn't seem to be a problem in this case. That way, if it doesn't work out with one person, there's always someone else in the basket to go out with and hope for the best. "If you limit yourself to just a few, you'll miss out on a lot of good people. And some of them are really yummy," Carrie says.

the flirting adventure

The next step after learning our flirting techniques and equipping ourselves with props is to hit the local bars and practice our new skills. The practice will come in the form of flirting assignments. Carrie will scope out the room and choose people for us to flirt with. She'll send us out to practice our triple fly-by rule and to use our flirting diplomas. And she will expect results.

But first, our group needs a clever ruse. "If anyone asks, we are from the Film Lovers Workshop. If they ask what that is, well, then you have your first opportunity to flirt," Carrie says.

Carrie looks around the room with relish. "I'm going to assign one of you to walk around with a name tag on your back," she says. People groan.

About half the group decides to pay another $45 for the adventure. If nothing else, the ones who go out are disadvantaged purely by the fact that Sunday night at eleven o'clock is not a popular time to find packed bars. Carrie's plan seems to be to have us practice our flirting skills on either heavy drinkers or the unemployed. She smiles her broadest grin yet and shepherds her minions out to their future of one-liners and gags. Mentally, I wish them luck.

If one person is becoming uppermost in your thoughts, if his society is more and more necessary to your happiness, if what he does and says seems more important than that of anyone else, it is time to be on your guard, time to deny yourself the dangerous pleasure of his company, time to turn your thoughts resolutely to something else.

FROM *The Young Lady's Friend,* BY MRS. H. O. WARD
(A Pseudonym for Clara S. J. Moore), 1880

II.

dating by the book

♥

♥

♥

John, thirty-nine, has been nursing a broken engagement for the past two weeks. His potential fiancée, Maggie, was worried John hadn't gotten over lingering issues from his prior relationship which lasted eight years, so she gave back the ring after two months. "I had stayed in my last relationship way too long even though I probably knew from the start it wasn't right," says John. During the time they dated, John and Maggie had broken up for a while, so John could get clear on what he wanted. Now he's ready to get married. Meanwhile, Maggie is dating a guy she met during their separation.

"I almost feel like I'm back to where I started years and years ago. It has been a long time since I dated," says John, who is from

New Jersey originally and now lives in Los Angeles. John admits he's at a loss when it comes to people. "I'm a shy person. I could never just go up to someone and start talking to her in a coffee-house, for example," he says. "If I walked up and she said no, I'd have to walk back to my seat alone. I could never do that." But John wants to be in a relationship. That he knows for sure.

Joan, an accountant in San Francisco, also wants to be in a re-lationship because she's ready to have kids, something that be-came an issue in a four-year romance that ended six months ago. "When we met, I was thirty-four and he was thirty-six," she says. "All my friends were single and all of his friends were single. But after three and a half years, I said it's time to have kids." Joan's boyfriend wasn't ready. They broke up. "Now he's dating a thirty-two-year old. He's had success dating." Joan is worried that her age and her biological clock will make dating a challenge. "I think there are a lot of guys who are in the emotionally same spot as I am but they are a little less committed to it because they don't need to be," she says. What to do?

aisles of advice

When I locate the shelves of dating-advice books in my local chain bookstore-cum-caffeine-provider, I am surprised to find that dating advice is lumped together in the psychology section with marital advice, self-esteem boosters, and books on personal productivity. There are books about flirting, books of pickup lines, books that look deep into our souls and ask why we're alone. There is a book on relationship soul-searching, and dating advice for almost every type of consumer—married, divorced, widowed, studious, lighthearted, confused, whimsical, desperate.

Among the best-selling books today is one that trades on Ivy League education and fears of being single after a certain age: *Find a Husband After 35 Using What I Learned at Harvard Business School*. Its author, Rachel Greenwald, uses her experience in marketing to distill her dating advice into fifteen chapters, with the assumption that dating is just a matter of effectively marketing ourselves. But first there is a sobering section devoted to explaining why women over thirty-five face increasing odds when trying to date. Changing bodies with pockets of cellulite, baggage from old relationships, dwindling numbers of single men, increasingly insular lifestyles—all are trotted out to put women in the properly depressed state of mind where they'll believe they can only succeed by aggressively attacking the dating world with marketing strategies heretofore reserved for telemarketers paid on commission. Market thyself or die alone.

The book uses marketing buzzwords to explain how "branding" ourselves is really just a matter of figuring out what sets us apart from all the other single people out there and using our unique attributes to present ourselves to the dating world at large. We are no different from a new toaster oven, which has to make use of attractive packaging, savvy advertising, and effective product placement. In other words, single women are supposed to tell everyone they know that they are interested in finding a husband and unleash this team of mass marketers on their friends and neighbors to set them up on dates. Dating becomes like hawking our wares on late-night cable, trying to drum up volume sales before our "product life cycle" is cut short by more cellulite or younger competition. This is what women seeking "expert" advice are faced with.

"A woman's age does scare a guy, and anyone who tells you otherwise is lying," says Joan. On a friend's advice, Joan signs up for Nerve.com, an online dating service, where she can "market" herself as a woman under forty who wants to have kids. Her friend, who is in her early thirties, had recently put a profile on Nerve and received fifty responses. Joan posts her profile and gets about ten responses. "There were a couple who seemed like such a good fit for me, and I watched how frequently they were online. So I knew they got my e-mails, but they never e-mailed me back," Joan says. "It's totally the age thing. People are thinking time clock when they see a woman is a certain age. I know that's an issue."

A few weeks later, when a colleague at a conference offers to introduce Joan to someone, she goes along with it. After all, she's just out of a relationship, looking to meet someone new. Her colleague knows a great man who has always been married to his career and now wants to have kids. He's forty-nine years old. The two go out on a few dates. He's okay, but Joan wonders about the odds of meeting someone her own age.

a history of advisers

Dating advice and etiquette books are not new. In the twelfth century, troubadours raised courtly love to an art form, one which

Andreas Cappelanus captured in his treatise, *The Art of Courtly Love* (translation by John Jay Parry). It's not known whether Cappelanus, chaplain to Countess Marie de Troyes, meant the work as a satire or a serious text. It broke ground by making a distinction between couples who were married and couples who were in love. This opened the door to romantic relationships between married women and the male suitors who would write songs and poetry in their efforts to woo them. The book provides advice on "in what manner love may be acquired," and tells lovers how to speak to each other across boundaries of class. Among the instructions on how to formally woo are warnings about getting involved with those with a proclivity for love with more than one partner: "Do not fall into the toils of such a woman because you cannot win her love no matter how hard you try." And for the men with similar wanderlust: "For he who is so tormented by carnal passion that he cannot embrace anyone in heart-felt love, but basely lusts after everyone he sees, is not called a lover but a counterfeiter of love and a pretender, and he is lower than a shameless dog."

By the early 1800s, etiquette was the underpinning of relationships, and advice books were plentiful, from grooming advice to interpretations of emotions. Columnists told single girls to make sure they wore deodorant lest their dates find out they have unpleasant smells. *A Female Beauty, as Preserved and Improved by Regimen, Cleanliness and Dress* (by Mrs. A. Walker) instructed women in 1840 on how to make themselves presentable enough to attract men. *The Fusser's Book* (Anna Archbald and Georgina Jones, 1904) advised men to "remember that all that chills you is not cold. In all probability she has been advised to refuse an invitation once in a while, or to be out occasionally when you call. Above all she may fear to give the impression that she is sitting at the telephone waiting for you to ring her up. Learn to distinguish between a slight frost and the cold spell that ushers in a whole winter of discontent."

Emily Post is one of the more well-known espousers of proper breeding in her 1922 tome, *Etiquette; "The Blue Book of Social Usage,"* [sic] but there were countless others, as appropriate for an era with prescribed courtship rituals: "The bachelor girl can on occasion go out alone with any unmarried man she knows well, if the theater she goes to, or the restaurant she dines at, be of conventional character," says Post. Early twentieth-century etiquette dictated that a man would call on a lady between four and seven in the evening. He'd receive permission before being introduced and would stay for a maximum of thirty minutes, never allowing a girl to carry anything when he was with her. As for the woman, it was improper to help a man off with his coat or to let a man call her by her first name unless they were engaged. Everyone who dated knew the rules and proceeded according to a measured set of expectations.

Authors have since doled out advice on everything from how to kiss to whether to go out on a blind date. In *No Nice Girl Swears,* Alice-Leone Moats warned women in 1933 that blind dates can be a source of boredom, especially when the date was arranged by a man's friend whose opinion will be based "upon whether he was once able to drink the entire University of Virginia under the table or he is a good football player."

with a grain of salt

Today's dating bookshelf runs the gamut from serious analysis to lighthearted advice. *Dating: A Singles Guide to a Fun, Flirtatious and Possibly Meaningful Social Life* (Amy Cohen and Hedda Muskat) tells readers to blast music and pamper themselves to get psyched up for dates. The advice on "53 ways to reel in fish" includes putting ourselves in public places, taking a class, going to clubs, gyms, and sporting goods stores, socializing at work, and going to trade shows, which are "packed with people who are usually ready to 'party.'" The book's authors, who were writers for the dating show *Love Connection*, seem to think that common sense can be packaged with cheerleader enthusiasm and sold as dating advice. I personally have never met people at a trade show who were even aware of the word "party" as a verb. Perhaps that's why they couch the book's title and promise only a "possibly meaningful" social life.

In San Francisco, a friend of Joan's suggests that the two of them host a singles party for friends of friends. "We're always saying to each other, 'I want to introduce you to a friend of mine,' and if all the single friends we know do that, maybe some of us will find dates." From that was born a "date my friends party," which would only allow single people to invite other single people to a bar for a Friday night happy hour. Joan sends out an e-mail to people she knows and encourages them to tell a friend. Joan gets 1,200 RSVPs and fills two bars with lines down the block. "I can't tell you the number of people who said, 'This was a great idea' and 'Thank you for doing this,'" she says. The average age at the party was thirty-five.

From this a business is born. Friends begin asking Joan to host another party. Bar owners offer drink specials and tell her they'll print up fliers and business cards for her to hand out. At a second party a couple of months later, Joan charges $5 a person and makes a killing. There are at least six hundred guests. But Joan notices that the crowd is distinctly younger. Within two weeks she hears about another singles concept party, also filled to capacity, that was hosted by someone else.

delving deeper

Then there are heavier psychological editions of books, like *Date Smart: How to Stop Revolving and Start Evolving in Your Relationships* (David D. ["The Dating Doctor"] Coleman and M. Richard Doyle). The book has such uplifting chapters as "Are You a Loser Magnet?" "Would You, Could You, Should You Date . . . You?" and "Why Your Relationships are Like a Revolving Door." In answer to the latter, the authors suggest self-sabotage, jealousy, and possession-obsession. Anyone who experiences fleeting self-esteem after reading about why dating success has been elusive can take heart in a special chapter called "It's Not all Your Fault." Who wouldn't want to jump up and look for a date right there in the bookstore, which, according to another book is an oft-overlooked mate-snaring spot.

And for those of us willing to admit our stupidity, there is *Dating for Dummies* by Dr. Joy Browne, which has advice on calming fears and "having a way cool time" on a date. Dr. Browne catalogs good places to meet new people, including neighborhood parties, grocery stores, bus stops, and spiritual centers and counsels against finding dates at the office, bars, online sites, and singles dances.

And onward down the advice aisle. The legions of advice givers today are in business because we are asking. We are demanding to know supposed insider information because we want to get the maximum amount of information with minimal effort. We want to get years of dating wisdom, which we'd pick up on our own just by going on lots of dates, only we want it distilled for us in six easy lessons or one hundred pages. But more than anything, we are simply at a loss about how to solve our dating dilemmas on our own. And we're hoping the authors of how-to manuals have figured out something we haven't.

"It takes an effort to meet people outside work," says John, living in Los Angeles. "I'm not from here. I don't have the built-in social network that I'd have if I lived in New Jersey, so it's hard to meet people." John has used online dating sites to find dates, mainly because he was able to make contact without having to go up to someone in person. But he hasn't met anyone yet who made it past a couple of dates.

"I'm worried I'll never meet anyone. I've never been in a worse place in my life," says John. "I'm not really sure how long it will take me to get over the rejection of the last relationship, to be able to date someone new. But I'm trying to be optimistic."

As for Joan, she's trying to decipher the mixed messages she's been getting from a man she's been dating on and off again for two months. They went out twice and had a really good time and then he left Joan a message. "He said, 'I had a really good time but I'm a little freaked out about how fast this is moving,'" says Joan. She goes out of town, and they make a date for when she gets back. "We went to a concert, and then he freaked out again," she says. "After heavily pursuing me, he couldn't deal."

After another short cooling-off period, he starts pursuing Joan again. "For the last three weeks I've talked to him every day and gone out with him twice a week. Now it's been four days since I've heard from him," says Joan. "I think he's freaking out again. And if that's the case, I'm done."

conclusion

love in a new era

♥

♥

♥

"By age thirty, I would have thought I'd be in a very different place," says Lori. Instead she's facing down blind dates set up by friends whose taste she regularly calls into question. "One guy had a lazy eye, and another guy my friend set me up with was a lawyer but I didn't find out until the night before that he has this problem—he doesn't have use of his hands," says Lori. "I don't want to sound superficial, but I'm thinking, My gosh, am I that bad that I would somehow fit with these people?"

Lori is a teacher in Newport Beach, a coastal town in Southern California where she moved after living in Portland, Oregon. The dating culture in Portland was markedly different. "At age twenty-three, most of the people were married and pursuing families. It felt kind of strange if you weren't married, like maybe there was something wrong," Lori says. Now, at thirty, with most of her friends married or in relationships, she feels the same way.

Lori has tried Internet dating through eHarmony, which requires members to take a personality test as part of its screening and doesn't reveal photos until there's some level of compatibility. Lori specifies that she'd like to meet someone who has never been married. "Sure enough, there is this person who says he meets all my criteria and then divulges he's divorced and has two kids," says Lori. "So, for all the screening, the service was not as personalized and selective as they made it seem." Lori has gone to church events but hasn't met anyone there. "It has the values and the community, but I don't really want to date someone if I'm going to church. How do I go up to someone in that situation?"

After her foray into online dating comes up empty, Lori considers signing up with "It's Just Lunch!" dating service and "8-Minute Dates" speed-dating events. "But something about me says it should be more natural. I feel like when it comes to that day when I have to use a service, I am a total loser," she says. "Maybe I need to keep trying different services. If I pay more money, is that going to guarantee I'm going to find the right person?"

Lori is surrounded by people who are married or in relationships. Her two sisters are married, and one of her good friends who has been single for a long time is now dating someone. "I'm the last one," Lori says. And that makes her reconsider paying a dating service to facilitate her search. "The idea that I'm paying money to try and meet someone feels like a failure," Lori says. "I want to take control and do what I can, but I'm leaving it up to fate at this point. Is that old-fashioned, thinking that someone in the supermarket will ask for my number?"

what our dating lives say about us

On some level, we all need a little encouragement. We all need to feel good about ourselves when we walk out the door, single, married, interested, or happily flying solo. And all of us occasionally need prompting to get out there in the first place. We can easily overlook this area of our lives because no one is holding us to a deadline or withholding our pay if we don't meet someone. Working is a necessity. Dating is not. Paying our bills and keeping our lives in order take precedence over finding someone to fall in love with. But the seminars, experts, and gimmicky events force us to take our social lives seriously. They instruct us to think about what we can do to meet one another, and they put us in situations where we can find other single adults. They shift our focus away from work and daily responsibilities and instruct us to put a priority on meeting one another and looking for love.

Our dating culture falls on the heels of the great self-help movement of the past several decades. We have been encouraged to seek help, to turn inward, to better ourselves. It makes sense that the self-esteem retreats and motivational seminars would ultimately dovetail with our dating lives. We are taught to work out our individual issues before we take on the issues of a relationship. It turns out there are as many self-proclaimed dating coaches as there are therapists, and many do double duty as both. They give us safe venues in which to socialize. They make it okay to be single and searching for love because they put us in the company of others who have the same desires. They make relationships feel attainable. Some of the people who help us become the surrogate for the community we've lost. Others prey on our fears and insecurities and make us think that our innate abilities aren't enough. On the whole, it is a case of caveat emptor combined with basic self-knowledge. Some of these methods work for some people. If they didn't, there wouldn't be success stories. But on the flip side, no one publicizes the stories of brilliant failure.

the urban phenomenon

Today, the large metropolitan areas where many of us live have several characteristics that put a strain on the traditional methods we use to meet one another and develop relationships. If we choose not to marry right after high school or college, when the available pool of single people our own age is nearly infinite, we have an increasingly difficult time tracking down the population of prospective dates with comparable interests. Our network gets smaller as we get further away from our college years. Many of us who live in large cities have moved there from elsewhere, so we're missing the network of friends and family to provide a basic social framework. And since that network is the way most of us meet new people, living in a place where it doesn't exist makes it harder to find people to date. We're then left dating people we meet through our jobs or through new circles of friends which can take years to develop.

We also must contend with the sheer volume of noise and

stimuli coming at us every day. We see billboards, we hear traffic, we listen to jackhammers gnawing at patches of sidewalk. We encounter people begging us to take surveys, asking for directions, or yelling at us through megaphones to follow their religious ways. Living in large cities requires a sophisticated screening mechanism to filter out the unwanted noise. But in the process of blocking out the excess and insulating ourselves in comfortable spheres where we can focus on our lives, we are often closed off to the very people we might want to date under less aggravated circumstances. We function in bubbles of comfort because we have to. Then in order to let potential dates into our bubbles, we are forced to use outside means.

Cities constrain our ability to meet one another by the sheer level of suspicion that urban life engenders. We hear about local crime each night on the news. It feels like almost everyone who lives in an urban area has either engaged in a friendly chat with a stranger who turned into a stalker or knows someone who has. We come to accept that part of the price of living in a dynamic center with culture, art, and entertainment is the risk that not everyone has noble intentions. Apply that thinking to dating and the result is a heightened level of distrust. Now, when someone talks to us in the grocery store we don't view it as a potential opportunity to meet someone new who shares our affinity for hothouse tomatoes. We view it as an intrusion into our personal space, an annoyance, and possibly even a threat. We're worried that the woman asking us if we know the difference between hydroponically grown lettuce and the organic variety is actually a deviant who is trying to distract us while she steals our wallet. We're afraid the man who observes that we're buying a lot of cat food is some potential stalker trying to figure out if we live alone with a cat. Most of us have tunnel vision when we run our errands around town, juggling mental lists and trying to get home with a minimum of intrusion from outsiders. An unexpected conversation at the video store can throw off our momentum and timing entirely. So we keep it brief, tell the nice person next to us that, yes, we liked *Dog Day Afternoon*, and move on with our lives without giving potential romance a second thought.

In our increasingly compartmentalized lives, the time for seeking romance may come later, post-workout, after errands, in the quiet space of our homes. Then we can log on to our computers and search for like-minded souls. Or looking at our single-serving dinner with disdain, we can leave a message for the dating service, hoping it will be the answer to our needs. We reach beyond our own circles to find people to date. We like the idea of Friendster because we know that anyone we meet on the site has some connection to someone we already know. It replicates the network of friends and family who can vouch for a potential date, just like they would do in a small community where everyone knows everyone else. Living in cities has robbed some of us of those close-knit communities, so we have to seek them out some other way. We are looking for the community of potential dates amid the enormity of our urban environment.

we have a business culture

Time is money. Efficiency is crucial. We want maximum return for minimal investment of our time and resources. We want data sets we can analyze and choices we can evaluate with tools we have at hand. Clearly, our jobs put demands on our time and energy. We are busy, and the dividend is less time to spend on our dating lives. But our jobs also affect the way we look at love. Risk and return. Opportunity cost. Net net. The values set forth by our working lives bleed into the way we evaluate and form new relationships.

The new dating goods and services reflect the way we've been trained to think during the business day. If we like the laws of probability, which tell us that the more people we meet, the greater chance of finding the love of our lives, there is speed-dating, which gives us maximum exposure to people in a target age range with a minimal investment of time. If we are accustomed to having a full set of facts at our disposal before we make decisions, Internet dating sites appeal because we can preselect for whatever characteristics we want in a potential date. If we rely on consultants and experts to do some of the legwork for us in evaluating problems and providing solutions, we can call upon matchmakers and advice givers who distill our search for dates into a manageable process. It's possible that the dating goods and services which seem outlandish on the surface are merely practical. They are there because we are asking for them.

attention-deficit daters

Never before has a generation lived at a time with so many new technologies to help us speed up everything we do. We can accomplish more than we ever could, from wherever we happen to be. That makes our lives easier in some ways, harder in others. It seems like every day there is some new device that we can get excited about. Not only are we accustomed to seeing people around us using the latest and newest personal data assistant with all its cool gimmicks, but the devices become part of our conversations, as we show off the ways we can do things faster, better, and more remotely.

How can a generation focused on doing things faster and more technologically come to terms with an antiquated process like getting to know someone in real time?

"We're wonderfully connected electronically and disconnected interpersonally," says Edward Hallowell, a Harvard University researcher and psychologist studying the effects of attention-deficit disorder. "We all contend with the fact that we don't know our neighbors or we don't see our friends as much as we'd like to." We are so excited by what the next new technologies can do that we are forgetting what their appropriate uses are. The problem is that not everything functions well at high speed. Like relationships.

Our business culture of deal making and demand for synergies and quick decisions shape our attention deficit. We apply the same techniques to relationships and expect them to conform to the business practices we're used to. "You end up saying, 'Okay, so you love me. What's your next point?'" Hallowell says.

We still want to believe it's possible to meet the love of our life without the new gimmicks that everyone thinks we should be using. No one wants to tell about meeting a husband or wife at a speed-dating event. There's still a fantasy of something more quaint, more traditional. That's what gives us hope.

history repeating itself

In some ways we've come full circle. Prior to the early twentieth century, men called on women at their homes, giving women control over which callers they'd keep company with and how long dates would last. When dating moved out of the home and into the public realm, it included entertainment which cost money, putting control in the hands of men who had jobs and could afford to pay. Online personal ads, speed-dating events, and self-esteem-boosting seminars again allow women to take the initiative and control the date. Women can vet the responses they get to their posted profile and accept callers only when they feel comfortable. There is no longer such formality in our dating rituals as visiting in sitting rooms, but the Internet has produced its own kind of etiquette.

And we haven't drifted as far as we think from 1930s dance-hall traditions where women were encouraged to dance with multiple partners in an evening. The old tradition in which men were supposed to compete for women has been replaced by the online phenomenon of a woman posting an Internet profile for the first time and receiving dozens of responses from men, all wanting to catch her attention. Different means, same dynamic. Maybe a singles mixer is simply the speakeasy of a new generation.

judging success

It is difficult to look at the modern services we use to prod our dating lives along and determine whether we are onto a magic bullet. For any service or innovation, there are success stories. Stories abound of men and women who found each other online, fell in love, and got married. Nearly every dating service boasts success stories of clients who met that way. There are satisfied graduates of relationship seminars who feel the tips they gleaned from their instructors were valuable in helping them find dates and develop relationships. Books make their way onto best-seller lists because readers believe they contain crucial words of wisdom that will solve their dating problems. But for every success story, there are countless failures. No one talks about the clients who are unlucky in love despite paying for matchmaking services or on-line dating memberships. It wouldn't be good advertising.

There's a temptation to say that anyone who discontinues a membership with a dating service, online or otherwise, does so because he or she has found a steady relationship. It would be easy to look at former clients of bricks-and-mortar dating services and assume that they were successfully matched and didn't need to pay for additional help. But in reality they're not all satisfied customers. Some merely don't want to spend more money on something that isn't working.

The value of our modern dating goods and services is difficult to quantify for other reasons. It's possible that people who succeed at meeting each other through particular types of dating services are the ones who are naturally drawn to them. Someone who is paying a lot of money to a dating service like It's Just Lunch! may be much more focused on finding a relationship than someone who is cruising a free dating Web site like Yahoo! Personals. Put two similarly focused paying individuals together and the success rate might be higher than two people who don't have money at stake.

Part of the success of dating goods and services lies in effective sorting. Two people who meet on a Hindu dating Web site will have a comfort level with people they meet there. As we push forward with our busy lives, it's hard to find people with similar attributes and interests merely in passing.

Another element of success stems from simple laws of probability. There is a greater chance of finding people we are compatible with if we meet a lot of people. The more people we are exposed to, the closer we can come to beating the odds. "It's a numbers game" is a mantra espoused across the board by the marketers of dating goods and services. It is a tenet of the advertising campaign for Match.com: eight million people are on its Web site—why aren't you? The concept could just be another way of saying, "Everyone's doing it." But behind that concept is the undeniable fact that if everyone is doing it, we have access to a lot more potential dates if we join up, too, than if we sit on the sidelines.

And then we have to stop and ask ourselves why. Why should it be that we have to suit up and join the dating race in order to meet one another? Are we too busy to find dates on our own or have we actually lost the desire to be part of the process? How many of us are really so socially inept that we need books of instructions or courses tailor-made to our dating flaws? Is technology providing us with more opportunities to find one another or is its very existence expanding the chasm between us? And if so, do we mind?

The fact of the matter is we're not ducks or chimpanzees. We don't function purely according to instinct and pheromones. We think. We overthink. We get insecure. We want solutions that promise to stack the odds. And we want results. Some of the goods and services that exist serve those needs. It isn't wrong to take advantage of them. It's a sign of the times that we have computers, consultants, and services at our disposal, so it's not a black mark on our culture to use them. Unless we're not happy with the process.

At the end of the day, if we bemoan the fact that we have to search through profiles to find one another, we may be telling ourselves something. Maybe the system isn't working. If we don't want to pay others to sort through potential dates or host events where we can socialize, we have to come up with more palatable alternatives. It's pretty hard to work an eighty-hour week in a city where we don't know anyone except our colleagues and expect a relationship to materialize out of the ether. We may have to make ourselves available to meeting someone on the subway or in the single-serving aisle of Whole Foods and fight the temptation to filter out the intrusion. Otherwise, we may find ourselves logging on to a lonely computer terminal at eleven o'clock at night in hopes of finding that like-minded soul who rides the same subway route and likes the same carrot-ginger soup we do. And they just may be there, surfing late into the night, looking for our profiles. We can only hope.